MW01505879

THE PROSPEROUS
WRITER'S GUIDE TO

FINDING
READERS

BUILD YOUR AUTHOR BRAND,
RAISE YOUR PROFILE,
AND FIND READERS TO DELIGHT

HONORÉE CORDER
BRIAN D. MEEKS
with *MICHAEL ANDERLE*

ALSO BY HONORÉE CORDER

*You Must Write a Book: Boost Your Brand, Get More Business
& Become the Go-To Expert*

*I Must Write My Book: The Companion Workbook to
You Must Write a Book*

<u>*The Prosperous Writer* book series</u>

*Prosperity for Writers:
A Writer's Guide to Creating Abundance*

Prosperity for Writer's Productivity Journal

The Nifty 15: Write Your Book in Just 15 Minutes a Day!

*The Prosperous Writer's Guide to Making More Money:
Habits, Tactics, and Strategies for Making a Living as a Writer*

———

*Business Dating: Applying Relationship Rules in Business
for Ultimate Success*

*Tall Order: Organize Your Life and Double Your Success
in Half the Time*

*Vision to Reality: How Short Term Massive Action Equals
Long Term Maximum Results*

The Divorced Phoenix: Rising from the Ashes of a Broken Marriage

*If Divorce is a Game, These are the Rules: 8 Rules for Thriving
Before, During and After Divorce*

The Successful Single Mom book series

The Miracle Morning book series

THE PROSPEROUS WRITER'S GUIDE TO
FINDING READERS

Build Your Author Brand,
Raise Your Author Profile
and Find Readers to Delight

HONORÉE CORDER
& BRIAN D. MEEKS
WITH MICHAEL ANDERLE

Digital ISBN: 978-0-9961861-9-3

Paperback ISBN: 978-0-9980731-7-0

Edited by H. Claire Taylor

Interior Design: Christina Culbertson, 3CsBooks.com

Honorée Corder
Brian D. Meeks
Co-authors of *The Nifty 15* & *The Prosperous*
Writer's Guide to Making More Money
with Michael Anderle

KINDLES FOR VETERANS PROGRAM

10% of the proceeds of this book are being spent to fund Michael Anderle's *Kindles for Veterans Program*. Thank you for helping us to provide Kindles and books by Indie Authors to the men and women who serve!

SPECIAL INVITATION

Many like-minded individuals have gathered in an online community to share ideas, render support, and promote accountability. When I first wrote *Prosperity for Writers*, I envisioned helping numerous writers shatter the belief that they must starve to survive. I had no idea what was in store, and the result is an amazing community of 700+ writers, authors, editors, and more!

I'd like to personally invite you to join the The Prosperous Writer Mastermind at HonoreeCorder.com/Writers and Facebook.com/groups/ProsperityforWriters where you will find motivation, daily support, and help with any writing or self-publishing questions.

You can connect with me personally on Twitter @ Honoree, or on Facebook.com/Honoree. Thank you so much for your most precious resource, your time. I look forward to connecting and hearing about your book soon!

TABLE OF CONTENTS

A Note from Brian & Honorée

To make a prosperous living, every writer and author needs more readers. We need our work to be discovered, bought, and read. And the more often, the better!

We can increase our writing's discoverability thanks to the introduction of self-publishing. Now, the sky's the limit, and we think that's awesome! Although some people moan about the increasingly crowded space, we say, *the more the merrier!* The people who write *prosperity* books are abundance thinkers, right? Right!

The available equal opportunity means more and more people will enter the self-publishing ring. You must do everything you can to stand out, get noticed, and *get your books read.* In fact, we want you to find as many readers as possible who will be delighted by your books!

It's not only about finding new readers. You need to find new readers who will become fans, and a select number who will become *super fans.* A super fan is someone who reads everything you've written.

There are lots of great books about finding more readers, and Honorée has read them all (some more than once), and Brian has spent countless hours in forums, on blogs, listening to podcasts, and testing his own theories to learn what works. We think they are all good and provide key advice you would benefit from. We've even listed our favorites in the Index.

WHY IS THIS BOOK DIFFERENT?

The steps we suggest you take to find new readers are in some ways similar to what you've quite possibly heard *ad nauseum* from other successful writers: do podcast interviews, blog, and build a list (all of which you can and should do, as soon as possible). You hear these same things over and over because these tactics are good, solid, appropriate, and effective. Because Honorée has spent almost two decades as a business coach and strategist, and Brian has spent a good bit of his life as a data analyst in the insurance industry, we have a unique perspective and some ideas we think you haven't heard before. Our main objective is to share some things we do that other people aren't doing *and*, hopefully, cause you to *think* and come up with your own spectacular ideas. The phrase "thinking outside the box" comes to mind here, because that happens to be what we do a lot of … especially when it comes to finding readers. We are constantly devising new, different, and dare we say, *ninja* ways for readers to discover our books.

Going the traditional publishing route hasn't worked for us, but thinking outside the box, going rogue, and becoming finding-readers-ninjas sure has! This book contains the ideas we are using that have worked and are continuing to work for us. We think these same strategies, either as we've executed them or as you customize them for yourself, can work for you, too.

WHAT'S NOT IN THIS BOOK

If you do what everyone else is doing (the aforementioned interviews, blogging, and list-building), particularly the successful people, you most likely are going to be successful, too. But there's a limit to how successful we can all be, if we are all replicating the same people. At some point, you will want to engage in some "Blue Ocean Strategy" (based on the book *Blue Ocean Strategy*: *How to Create Uncontested Market Space and Make the Competition Irrelevant* by

Renée Mauborgne and W. Chan Kim). Lasting success increasingly comes not from battling competitors but from creating "blue oceans" of untapped new market spaces ripe for growth. Said another way, swimming out to a new part of the ocean and blooming there. To that end, we're not going to discuss the strategies everyone is already doing past this point. After a quick discussion about preparation, we're going to jump right to sharing the *other* things we're doing to promote our books and increase discoverability.

Does all of this still sound good? Okay, then, let's go!

YOUR PLAN TO FIND READERS

FIRST THINGS FIRST

We promise we are going to blow your noodles when we share the ninja strategies in Section Two. But never ones to put the cart before the horse, it would be a disservice to you if we simply shared tactics and didn't help you set the stage for successfully executing them. Section One will help you define your plan for finding new readers, and Section Two contains the strategies that work best for us. These are strategies that will either work great for you, too, or help nudge your creative juices to define some that will yield you new super fan readers. Section Three shares lessons and ideas from Brian, and Section Four has a practical plan for moving you toward the success you desire.

Whether you have a fiction or non-fiction book, why on Earth would you want to go to all the trouble of finding new readers in unique and out-of-the-box ways? Being a ninja is hard work; it requires determination, endurance, strength, and flexibility. We're not in the business of making you guess what works, because we're on the clock here. People must be exposed to you and your books several times before what they see registers. And they'll need to hear about you maybe even a few more times before they act (if ever).

When you play your cards right, put your book into the right hands, you could soon experience the power of going viral. There's nothing like, "You have *got* to read this book!" to encourage someone to read it. But you must get the book into the hands of that first person who thinks your book rocks and should jump to the top of the pile. The reason this is important is because the number one way a book is discovered is through a personal recommendation. The challenge is getting your books in the hands of enough people in order to allow the buzz to occur.

You might not have heard the story of the first book in the Harry Potter series, arguably *the most profitable book in history*. Well, then-single mom and aspiring author J.K. Rowling tried to sell her book to dozens of publishing houses and they all said no. Who's crying now? It wasn't until an agent owed a friend a favor and tossed the book to his daughter, that the book got discovered. Why? Because that young lady voraciously read the book in less than a day, and wanted to know where the second book was.

Yes, dear reader, getting your book in the hands of the right readers who are delighted by it is the ticket you need to find other readers.

The Plan

Honorée here.

I spent almost two decades as a business and executive coach, and coaches are known for advocating for great goals and the solid plans that support their attainment. Now, when I first began, my plan consisted of *identify seven things to do every day to market my book* and I did them. Not much of a plan, really, in retrospect. More random action taken with my fingers crossed.

I missed a very important aspect of a great plan: the goal. What did I ultimately want from marketing my books? Money? Sure! But how much? I didn't say. Sales? Well, duh, but I didn't identify *how many* I wanted, so theoretically I would've been happy with any result, which is absolutely not the case.

I took non-directed action without an outcome because I didn't take the time to think it through. Lucky for me, even though I didn't know what I didn't know, my tactics worked. Lucky for you, I paid the "stupid tax" you don't have to pay! Even without a strategy, I was successful based upon my non-identified outcomes. I made enough money to feel like my time, money, and energy were well spent. But I often wonder: *What if I had based my tactics in some solid strategy? What if I'd known to have a solid plan with action steps based on the goals set forth in the plan?*

You're reading this book because you want to find more readers, as easily and as quickly as possible. In order to do that, you're going to need a plan, a goal or three, and action items that support the goals and the plan. Make sense? Then let's get on with it, shall we?

Your Action Plan

To be truly successful, you need to have what I didn't know to have: a plan that consists of goals and action items. I'm going to walk you through my process for determining my goals and the corresponding action items. I've got a blank, downloadable Plan for you here (HonoreeCorder.com/FindingReaders), and you'll see an example in Section 4.

What Do You Want?

The first step in any action plan is to determine what exactly you want from your writing. If you have a book or book series in mind, knowing your desired outcome is key. There are only two logical outcomes, or goals, that makes sense: you need to sell "x" number of copies, or you want to make "x" amount of money. If you've read my book, *Prosperity for Writers,* you know I advocate for identifying your monthly nut (the amount of money it takes to live your life every month) and then multiplying that number by 1.5, which is your financial income goal. If you haven't yet read that book, you'll probably want to get it to use as a resource and basis for expanding your writing business via expanding your prosperity consciousness.

For your Plan, I strongly suggest you set two goals, one based upon the other. Your financial income goal and the number of sales you need to need to make to achieve it.

I'm going to use $10,000 a month, or $120,000 per year as an income goal. If you've made $120,000 at any point in your life, this probably sounds like a solid number. But if you saw that number and your head exploded, let me present the number to you in another way: $328.77 per day. I like round numbers, so instead of $328.77, we're going to use $330.00 and give you an immediate raise to $120,450 per year. (You're welcome.)

A daily income of $330.00 per day is the sale of just ninety-five (95) $4.99 e-books on Amazon with their 70% royalty rate. You'll need a large catalog of books to reach that number, and it might take you quite some time to write as many books as it takes to sell a combined total of 95 e-books per day. But while the clock is ticking on the amount of time you have to read and get value from this book, there is no shot clock on how quickly you must get to $330 a day, or whatever you've determined your number to be. While, of course, you want to get there as quickly as possible, it will take as long as it takes and I'm here to tell you *it's okay for it to take as long as it takes.*

Goal-setting: Pull out your journal and determine the amount of money you want to make in a year (it could be your monthly nut times 1.5, or perhaps you just want to make enough to take a fantastic vacation every year—completely up to you). Divide that number by 365. (Note: Your income is not taking days off, holidays, or even vacation time. The idea is that you can make money every single day, rain or shine, work or no work … even while you are sleeping! Just choose the number you truly desire to make. Ultimately, it is the activity you take on the days you work that influences the outcome and timing.)

Your annual number is your Goal #1. Your daily number is your Goal #2.

What you've got now are your target numbers.

ACTION ITEMS

In Section Two, Brian and I give you a list of our best strategies. You can take the best from them and add some of your own. We can surmise you're chomping at the bit for us to get down to it. I, too, am ready for you to dive into it, but there's one more thing for us to cover first.

YOUR RETURN ON TIME INVESTMENT

Brian, my co-author for several books in *The Prosperous Writer* series, can ensure that the action items you choose are getting you the best ROTI (return on time investment). Before I hand it over to Brian, let me give one quick example of bad vs. good ROTI:

- Doing a book signing, or even "going on a book tour" sounds like a big, fun, sexy thing to do. The problem is, unless or until you have a private jet and own properties in 50 major cities, you're going to endure an unending string of hotel rooms, commercial airline travel (which, these days, is *super fun*

… not!), and eating all of your meals out. Yup, this is a fantastic adventure for a few days or weeks, but at some point, don't you just want a hot shower in your own bathroom, a home-cooked meal *in your own home,* and to fall into a deep, cozy sleep in your own bed? I know I do! And all of this to sell a few dozen or maybe even a few hundred copies at best. Gross profit: $200-$500. Net profit: less than $0 because you probably have a huge balance on your American Express Card. (Don't leave home without it.) Yup, you guessed it— bad ROTI.

- Doing a teleseminar or podcast interview. From the comfort of your own couch (and yes, you can still shower, eat, and sleep in your own bed with no interruptions, boarding passes, or over-priced room service), you can talk to countless people around the world about your book and why it's wonderful. Someone can't attend? No problem! They can listen with the same device they carry in their back pocket or purse at all times: their phone … which also happens to double as an audio device that can deliver your interview and even your audiobook. ROTI = *awesome.*

Now I'm going to hand the mike to Brian and let him weigh in with some terrific thoughts I know you'll enjoy:

BRIAN HERE.

I'd like to share an ROTI I made recently where the return was actually close to 400%.

Let me explain. I love data and, as such, I'm constantly aware of when I'm letting time slip away. When I've added something on my daily to-do list that I'd rather not do, like, *Write some new ad copy for five ads*, I have an investment of one hour. I can come up with clever copy fairly quickly and I've done it enough that when I see that item on the list, I know it means I need to put my butt in the chair for about two back-to-back episodes of *Archer* (with commercials).

There's a problem, though, a secret time expense that can go unnoticed but is costing you (and me) thousands of dollars a year in lost productivity. I'll tell you more about that in a second, but first, let me tell you what I did to address the one-hour issue.

Writing ad copy isn't as bad as cleaning the gutters (which I always put off until the very last possible day of the fall when the temperature is miserable and the wind is about twenty miles per hour out of the north). It's something that I don't have to do. I could train someone else to bang out the pithy pitches.

That's what I did. I hired an assistant. Her name is Laurie, and she's awesome. She's been writing my ad copy for several months now and, because she has a different voice from mine, has created a lovely new perspective for the ads.

I had originally imagined that paying Laurie to do one hour of my work for me would have a 100% ROTI. I would get rid of the hour of work I needed to do and free it up for something else. I was *wrong!* The ROTI is probably closer to 400%.

"But Brian, aren't you the son of a mathematician? That doesn't seem possible."

Here's the deal. I didn't notice it at first, but when I began transferring the daily list items (ad copy and other things I didn't want to do) to Laurie, I had MUCH more time than just the hour she was working. It was closer to freeing up five hours.

Not everyone who reads this is going to have a problem with procrastinating when they don't want to do something, but for me, it was a bigger issue than I imagined. When I would get to *write ad copy* on my to-do list, the first thing I would do is go get a new bottle of water (or some other bottled drink that I had run out of, because that meant a trip to the store). I'd return with my snack item and check in with Facebook. Oh, what about Twitter? I'd better see if I have any new emails. Wait, stop everything, it's been three minutes since I updated the feed on

Facebook—I'd better get back there. Whew, nothing major happened, but I did see a post making a reference to a movie I've seen a dozen times and just loved. I had better watch it again (now).

Okay, so after a trip to the store, various social media check-ins, a movie, and possibly a brief nap, I'm ready to write some ads. THIS is how I behaved with most of the horribly unpleasant tasks (in my mind) on my list. The moment I had Laurie doing them, I saw my daily productivity go through the roof. I got to work on the things I wanted to be doing.

That's how you get 400% ROTI.

Now it's time for Honorée to close the ROTI loop and get you excited about your action plan.

Hi again! Honorée here.

Sometimes an identified action item that sounds fun and amazing is actually a horrendous waste of time and you'll wish you had made up some lame excuse, like food poisoning or your cat needed an emergency appendectomy, so you could have been spared the torture of whatever thing you're stuck doing. (Or is that just me? Apparently not, after reading Brian's account above.) And, sometimes an identified action item is truly fun and amazing. My point is this: you must not only identify action items, you should do them all while noticing if they are worth your time, money, and effort.

11

And let me rant about *time* for just a minute. It seems to me most people are confused. They are under the illusion it would be better to spend their time instead of money because they "can't afford to spend money." But here's the truth: they have it backward, and just maybe, so do you! You do *not* have an unlimited amount of time. In fact, I want to thank you for spending your time reading this book, because once time is spent, you can never get it back. Money, on the other hand, can come at any time, and if you're on my prosperity wavelength at all, you believe that when you spend money, even more money is on its way to you. I digress, yet I feel like it's an important point to make. Let me say it another, more positive and less snarky way. *Be doubly as mindful of how you spend your time as of how you spend your money.* You can always get more money, but time is finite, and once it has been spent, it is gone forever.

End of rant.

Now that Brian and I have shared our thoughts on money and time and assume we are all on the same page, let's dive into my favorite ninja tips and strategies for finding readers.

Ninja Ways to Find Readers

Honorée here.

As I mentioned, I engage in all of the usual ways to find readers (the aforementioned podcast guesting, blogging, and list building). When I wrote my first book, I heard Mark Victor Hansen say he and his co-author Jack Canfield did seven things every day to promote their book. And my thought was, *What a great idea!* Not one to, at least initially, try to improve on a great idea, I wrote down the seven things they did every day and did them myself.

While my very first book, *Tall Order!*, was "getting published" (read: being printed), I got busy doing my seven daily book marketing activities. That was in 2004, so I can't begin to tell you what all seven were back then, but I do remember that one of them was to get featured in local newspapers and magazines. I would no sooner do that today than I would wash my own car! But it worked— I was featured in *Las Vegas Magazine* and a couple of other local newspapers and publications and, I won't lie, it was pretty cool. But today, local magazines or newspapers don't exist in abundance, and even when they do, I don't read a single one (or know anyone who does). Just sayin'.

Before I dive into my favorite ninja strategies, I want to tell you why, *thirteen years later*, I'm still making a list of at least seven things to do every day to market my books and find new readers.

The printer I used to "publish" the original version of *Tall Order!* had a minimum print run of 1,000 books. But the cost per book was virtually cut in half if I ordered 5,000 instead, which, being the fiscally responsible person I am, is exactly what I did. Then I had a "holy shiznit" moment when I realized 5,000 books were going to show up on my doorstep (which, as it turned out, was only twenty-seven smallish boxes and wasn't nearly the truckload I thought it would be) in five to six weeks. With visions of my three-car garage turned into a sad version of a storage unit, I knew I needed to get to selling, and fast! Thus, the to-do list of seven things.

But here's where it gets interesting (and awesome). Because I was focusing on finding readers for my books in multiple ways every day, *I found them!* In fact, while the original order of 5,000 was in production, I sold 11,000 copies. New problem: I didn't have enough books coming! Yes, I sold one copy here, one copy there, five and ten copies here, and twenty-five copies there. But I also sold a few batches of a thousand copies, and even received one order for 3,000 copies. The larger orders I sold at a discount, yet I still grossed over $100,000 before I ever saw one book in print. For those of you who are curious about how I sold 11,000 copies, you can read more about this at HonoreeCorder.com/11000.

Now, I'm of a generation that thinks it's gauche to brag or talk numbers. I know some people like to do income reports and brag about how much they are making, and that is just not my style. But I think it's important that I pull back the curtain just a little so A) you know I'm legit and B) you are encouraged to make your own list and get started right away. (Is it working? I'd love to know. Send me an e-mail at Honoree@Honoreecorder.com and tell me!)

Because of my initial and early results with my first book, now, more than twenty books later, I am constantly looking for new, unique, and most importantly, effective ways to find new readers. I don't let the grass grow under my feet and don't think you should either.

I suggest you make a master list of the strategies you can find, and then, one by one, a few at a time (or even seven at a time) give them a try. In fact, as one of this book's bonuses, we've created the Master Book Marketing Strategies List you can access here: HonoreeCorder.com/FindingReaders.

Make sure you give each strategy you try long enough to work, adjust them as the market changes, or as you see them working or not working. Sometimes strategies require some time to take hold, and some you'll have to alter to fit your specific type of book. Some will work better with some books than others. Some will work for a while, and then become ineffective. Pay close attention to what is working, what isn't working, what is no longer working, and see if you can change or adjust them so they work well for you in your book's case.

BRIAN HERE.

Before you can continue reading, I think it's important that I mention that *data* is crucial and you will want to track your data so you know for sure if a strategy is working for you or not. Keep track of the marketing strategies you're using and where your book sales are coming from. This will provide you with incontrovertible evidence of what is, and is not, working. And one more quick thing: don't make the mistake of quitting too soon, before you can judge results. It can take several days, or even weeks, before you can truly judge whether any of the strategies you're using are working.

Now here's Honorée again.

Let's Get Ninja

The time has finally come to reveal my favorite strategies. If you've skipped straight to this part (and who could blame you?), go ahead and read. But then start again at the beginning so you are executing from a solid place with an excellent plan, okay?

Here are a few of the "in real life" strategies (a.k.a. off-line) I've been told are leading edge and pretty cool (please note that online strategies are coming up, too!):

Give books away.

The number one way someone finds out about a book they just "have to read" is because someone tells them about that book. I suggest giving away as many books as you can, as fast as you can, as soon as you can. *Tall Order!* is now thirteen years old, but if you haven't heard about it before right now the book is new to you. My point being that even a book that's been around 100 years is new to the person who hasn't heard about it yet. If you have the opportunity to give someone a book, by all means, *give them your book!* Giving away copies of your book can cost as little as a dollar or as much as a few dollars. In the case of my original *Tall Order!* (2004 version) book, I purchased those first 5,000 copies for $4,000, a cost of eighty cents per book. If you're new or just starting out, spending even a few dollars over and over might be too much for your pocketbook to bear. I get it, I'm fiscally responsible, remember? Make no mistake, your book is not just a book; it is your business, or at least a revenue stream of your overall business. To that end, I thought up a few ways to gain exposure for my books that cut the cost to a fraction of a cent in both of the following cases:

USE POSTCARDS. — Pastors + churches?

When I published *Vision to Reality* in 2013, I had postcards made with just the book cover on one side of the postcard, and left the opposite side in the same style as a regular postcard. This enabled me to send a postcard and ask the recipient *Would you like a copy of this book?* They had the option of using the QR code on the message side of the postcard to purchase the e-book, paperback, or audiobook directly from Amazon, or they could visit my website (also listed) to purchase a signed copy from me. Of course, seeing the postcard wasn't limited to just the recipient. Anyone who saw the postcard could indeed be intrigued enough to look up the book and get a copy if it was right for them. Since then, I have also had postcards made for *If Divorce is a Game, These are the Rules.* My lovely assistant, Christina, sends out a few a week to divorce attorneys, with the message "to request a complimentary copy of this book, feel free to email Christina@HonoreeCorder.com and we'll be happy to send you one." The postcard is a low cost and effective way to raise awareness about the book, and has resulted in another fun result: large-quantity purchases and even custom-printed copies.

BOOKMARKS ARE AWESOME, TOO.

For *The Successful Single Mom* and *The Successful Single Dad* books, I created bookmarks that could be shipped along with the original printed copies of the book. Because the book pre-dated CreateSpace, I had purchased thousands of copies and distributed them on Amazon through their Amazon Advantage program (http://tinyurl.com/h4xbnl3). But as luck would have it, I not only changed addresses, I also got married, changed my name, and moved to another state. Not very strategic on my part, and while each one presents its own problem, all of them combined made my head spin. All the contact information (including the website information) listed inside the book became null and void. Rather than creating the world's largest book bonfire, I decided to get creative and figure out a way to update the info without wasting the book. I used bookmarks with my updated information and a QR code and inserted them inside the front cover. The bookmarks also gave a special offer and enabled me to sell the books (instead of using them in place of firewood). Bookmarks can also be mailed, left in strategic places, even used in giveaways.

Both postcards and bookmarks are incredibly cheap. Postcards run about $150 for 2500 (and it takes quite awhile to give away 2500 postcards, even with fierce intention and determination)! Bookmarks are equally as inexpensive – around $25-45 for 1000 at http://waxpaper.interfirm.com. They offer multiple size and color options, as well as printing on one or two sides of your bookmark!

STAMPS.

I recently got stamps for *You Must Write a Book, Prosperity for Writers,* and *Vision to Reality.* They are full front covers of both books, made thumbnail size and in stamp form—the cost is the price of a stamp plus a tiny bit more for printing. I get compliments on them every time I use them, and again, they aren't limited to the intended recipient's eyeballs. Anyone who sees them will most likely take notice because unique stamps are rare and eye-catching. You might even find yourself getting back in the habit of writing daily thank-you notes! You can get yours from Zazzle. com (which is one of two providers to USPS.com). They also make great gifts for authors, too.

"Cult of (insert your name here)" swag.

My wonderful and encouraging friend, Amy Teegan, first coined the phrase "Cult of Honorée" and immediately Christina (my director of operations) had mugs made with my company logo and turned the phrase into a hashtag: #cultofhonoree. While I find this hysterical, creating my own hashtag or swag isn't something I would have done myself. However, recipients of the mugs use, love, and cherish them (and post them on Instagram with #cultofhonoree). Which is most likely exactly what will happen if you create some of your own. You could use your book covers on mugs, T-shirts, or even book bags and give them away when (1) someone leaves a five-star review for your book, (2) someone sends you a handwritten note telling you they love you and/or your books, (3) you hold a drawing or a contest, or (4) you have a book signing.

(Brian here: I use my #cultofhonoree mug every day.)

Starbucks coffee shops.

Starbucks provide their very own unique and wonderful opportunity for authors. Not only can you write there and have snacks and drinks at your disposal, you can utilize them to increase discoverability, *and* find new readers! Have you ever noticed each one has either a lending library or a newspaper basket—or both? When you're finished with your newspaper, you can leave it on your table for the next person, or place is in the basket near the "newspapers for sale" rack for reuse. Well, who said only newspapers go in those baskets? Not me! I don't visit a Starbucks anywhere on my travels (even if it is to one of the two locations that are less than three minutes from my home) without leaving at least one of my books behind. Sometimes if I don't have a book, I will add a postcard or a bookmark to the information board. My local Starbucks love me for it (and always have a Venti Youthberry tea with three Splenda at the ready when they see me coming). I was just in Miramar Beach, Florida, over spring break. Of course, my family headed to Starbucks each morning after breakfast, and, of course, I made friends with the baristas. Among them was a single mom who was so stoked I was bringing a book along to leave behind. If your book is nonfiction, it might find the perfect reader at the perfect moment and provide them with the solution they've been seeking. If your book is fiction, it might just find the perfect reader at the perfect moment who needed to get lost in the story only your imagination could provide. I just got five new subscribers to my list in the past week from Baton Rouge, Louisiana ... one of the places we stopped both ways on our trip. Coincidence? Who knows, but I don't think so!

SEEDING THE MARKET

"Seeding the market" is what I call leaving my books, postcards, and bookmarks pretty much everywhere I go. More than two or three *dozen* times I've received an email from someone telling me they stumbled upon my book and usually, at just the moment they needed it most.

Am I making money directly from the books and postcards I leave behind or send? Not necessarily. But is it possible, probable even, that the person who finds the book might purchase another book, one of my courses, hire me as their coach, or even buy an e-book copy of the book they found? *Yes.* All of the above have happened, making my seeding strategy incredibly effective. About two years ago, I sent a box of *The Successful Single Mom* book (box count: 128) with my in-laws on a fifteen-state tour. They drove from Louisiana to Nova Scotia and back … leaving my books at Starbucks all along the way. A win for Starbucks (repeat customers!), a win for Starbucks customers (buy a coffee, get a book!), and a win for me, who found new readers in new places with a relatively small time and monetary investment.

Doctors' offices.

At least once a year, my doctor tasks me with having my blood tested. I leave my books in his office and at the clinic. My husband and daughter also find themselves in doctors' offices (and dentists and massage therapists and nail salons) at various times throughout the year. You can bet your sweet self my books, bookmarks, and postcards are left behind each and every time.

AIRPORTS AND AIRPLANES.

As a corporate trainer and speaker, I have occasion to travel several times a year. In addition, my husband and daughter are always up for an adventure. And when it's done via the friendly skies, I'm provided with yet more opportunities (as are you!) to seed the market. Leave a book in the seatback pocket, a postcard in the airline magazine, a bookmark in a book similar to yours in the airport bookstore.

BOOKSTORES.

Speaking of bookstores, until Amazon recently opened bookstore number one in Seattle to showcase its bestselling titles (congratulations to my business partner in *The Miracle Morning* book series, Hal Elrod, for being one of the featured titles!), I was convinced brick and mortar bookstores were not long for this world. Now, I'm not so sure. But what I have been doing for years, because I have never been "one of the chosen few" whose books were distributed to bookstores everywhere, is put my books in bookstores exactly where they would be on the shelf if they *were* distributed to bookstores everywhere. Just one copy. Spine out—I mean, I'm not paying for the front cover facing space. When I go back a couple of days later, you know what? Nine times out of ten, the book *is not there*. Either someone found it and tried to buy it, or someone at the store found it and, well, I don't know what exactly. But on dozens of occasions, again, I have received a call from bookstores as small as the mom and pop independent store in Milwaukee, Wisconsin, to the Barnes and Noble I can hit with a rock from my front door wanting to know how they can *get more books*. "Someone tried to buy your book. We're not sure how it got here, but we couldn't sell it and had to let them have it. But we'd like to order some. Can we?" Ummm, *yes!*

FAMILY AND FRIENDS AS YOUR MARKETING TEAM.

My husband, Byron, has an office at We Work, a co-op work space where he rents an office and shares common areas. A few times a week, he leaves any or all of my business books in the common areas or conference rooms or even private phone booths for the next user to find. He also leaves behind postcards and bookmarks at his regular Starbucks. A few of my friends travel quite a bit for work, and for those who are (not yet) authors, I give them a book or two and some postcards to help me with my cause.

ONLINE NINJA STRATEGIES FOR FINDING READERS

Readers are everywhere, and you can be, too. What do I mean? Well, in addition to leaving physical books in actual places, you can leave digital breadcrumbs for your future readers to find. Make sure you do some (all!) of the following action items to find more readers.

PUBLISH IN ALL FORMATS.

While each of us has our preferred method of reading, there are readers who will only read physical copies of a book. People who travel quite a bit love the portability of their Kindle or iPad for taking lots of books along for the ride (and easy and instant accessibility). The newest way to consume a book is, without question, the audiobook—and it is quickly becoming a fan favorite. As the author, you don't have to be monogamous to one format. In fact, it behooves you to provide them all.

Why? Because, as I mentioned, different readers prefer different formats. Some readers like to own all formats of their favorite books! Having your book in physical format is great for those who like to highlight, mark specific pages or passages, or refer to their book. A digital book usually costs less and is portable. Audiobooks are gaining in popularity and with Amazon's Whispersync feature, your reader can read a great story before going to bed, and continue "reading" right where they left off as they work out, get ready, or even drive to work the next morning.

In addition, you are considered even more serious about your author status with multiple formats. When all three formats show up on your Amazon or Apple sales pages, you tell the world, *I am a serious author, you should read my book!* We won't go off on a tangent to discuss how to get your audiobooks produced, but keep this in mind: just as we've advocated producing professional books, we know a professionally produced audiobook is just as important.

E-BOOK–SPECIFIC PROMOTIONS.

While there's nothing quite like giving away a physical book, don't underestimate the power of giving away your e-book as well. Here are just two options:

GIVE AS A GIFT.

Amazon's sales pages offer the "Give as a Gift" function (about two inches beneath the price). You can give the book to the recipient of your choice, all you need is their email address. You can forward the gift email or print and personally deliver it to the recipient. You can also choose the date of delivery (think birthday, anniversary, or the holiday of your choice). Finally, you have the option of personalizing a message to the recipient.

MAKE IT AVAILABLE TO ALL!

Just as I think you just can't lose by giving your physical books away, sharing your e-books can help you find more readers. You can make the book available via a special page on your website, or even in your own website store. And, if you don't yet know about Bookfunnel.com, you're in for a treat. This low-priced option for providing your e-book in the format of the recipient's choice is simply genius. All you have to do is upload the PDF, .mobi, and .epub versions of your book, provide the link to whomever you choose, and they will get the book to read on their preferred device, in their preferred format. BookFunnel is my choice for sharing with each of my books' Advanced Reader Team (if you want to join mine, visit HonoreeCorder.com/ateam).

HOST A GIVEAWAY.

Amazon has a cool program that allows anyone to give away any book by hosting a giveaway. Amazon Giveaway allows you to run promotional giveaways to create buzz, reward your audience, and attract new followers and customers. You'll find it all the way down on the left side of the page, after the reviews.

Before I share the *how-to's* of the giveaway option, let me offer some advice: I suggest using this option to help other authors. Giving away your own book is, indeed, a fantastic idea and will help you find more readers. But I love the idea of tapping into the karmic forces of the Universe, so why don't you find someone else's book and give it away?

In fact, this book was already completely written and ready for editing when Michael Anderle gave away ten copies of our book *The Prosperous Writer's Guide to Making More Money*. People loved entering the giveaway, Michael had some super fun "you're a loser!" messages for those that didn't win, *and many of the people who didn't win bought the book anyway.* Best of all, Michael made us love him even more (if that was possible) because he paid it forward.

I was inspired by Michael, and I gave away five copies of Chris Syme's book *Sell More Books with Less Social Media*. If you love a book, give it away! By all means, give yours away too. Perhaps you'll find lots of other people will be inspired to share your books with their connections and you can help each other.

Now, let's get to the how-to:

- You start by selecting the book you want to give away; then how many you want to give away. Next, you select your giveaway type (this is where it can get fun, too):

- Sweepstakes. (Winners will be randomly selected after giveaway ends.)

- Random instant win. (Host selects chances of winning, winners are randomly selected.)

- Lucky number instant win. (Host selects "lucky number," winners selected by entry order. You'll select a number between 2-500.)

First-come, first-served. (Host selects number of prizes and everyone wins.)

You have the option to grow your audience by requiring some sort of hoop they must jump through to participate. Here are your choices:

- Follow the author of the book on Amazon

- Follow you (the host) on Twitter

- Tweet a message

- Watch a short video (specifically, an Amazon shorts video)

- Watch a YouTube video

- Answer a poll (my personal favorite, because you get to choose both the winning and losing messages—this is where your sense of humor can come into play)

Next, you select how long the giveaway will run. You have the option, if you are an Amazon.com seller, to promote the items listed in Seller Central. Your giveaway can be made public or by invitation only. Finally, giveaways are limited to the 50 United States and District of Columbia.

Once you've made all of those decisions, you'll design your Giveaway Page. You'll need:

- A giveaway title
- Your name
- An image of what you're giving away (simple to grab a screen shot of the book)
- Welcome message (for this one and the next two, *have fun* and let your sense of humor come out)
- Win page message
- Lose page message
- Advanced option: allow people to share the giveaway (or not)

Once your giveaway is processed, you'll receive an email confirming the giveaway purchase, and another with the URL to use to share it.

Giveaways are fun, build good karma, and help find readers. I, for one, am going to be hosting them as often as I can! What about you?

AUDIOBOOK-SPECIFIC PROMOTIONS.

I think audiobooks are the future of books, and you can definitely find more readers with audiobooks. Try these on for size:

- Share clips of your books on social media. Just a few words about your book, along with the image that auto-populates with your link, can spark someone's interest.

- Add your audiobooks to your Goodreads book list (see more, below).

- Audible offers a bounty of $50 for the author who brings new subscribers to their platform. While there are many people who have discovered audiobooks, there are tens of millions of people who haven't. Share your free audiobooks with others, and you'll find listeners for your other books as well.

• Use your promotional audiobook codes to share your book. When you publish on Audible, you get twenty-five free promotional download codes to share as you wish. You can share them through your social media, newsletter, blog, or even a site like Audiobookboom.com.

ADD YOUR BOOK TO YOUR EMAIL SIGNATURE.

You can just add "author" underneath your name (with a link to your Amazon Author Page), or you can add an image of your book cover or covers. You can choose to add a link to your free two-chapter opt-in of your book (see example here – HonoreeCorder.com/YouMustSample), or just link to the site where you sell the most books.

WAIT, YOU DON'T HAVE AN AMAZON AUTHOR PAGE?

I'm always surprised when an author doesn't have an Amazon Author Page. You can get yours at AuthorCentral.Amazon.com. Author Central is where sophisticated readers go to vet a newly-discovered author. It takes just a few minutes to add your professional author photo, a bio that shows your personality, and links to your website and blog. Most important: claim your books in all formats. The minute your book goes live on Amazon, hop over to

Author Central and claim your book. Be sure to check out Dave Chesson's article How to Setup Amazon Author Central and Your Author Page here: https:// kindlepreneur.com/amazon-author-central-page/.

AND WHILE YOU'RE AT IT ... WHAT ABOUT GOODREADS?

Goodreads is owned by Amazon, however they don't cross-promote when it comes to author information. Goodreads is a rich source of new readers. Here are just a few ways you can use it:

Goodreads is an online social network specifically for authors and readers, with more than twenty-five million members (that's a lot of readers!). Goodreads has just one job: it helps people find the next book they want to read. Think of it as Pandora or Spotify but for books.

Goodreads readers list the books they have read, along with their star rating (and the option to leave a full review). You can also connect with your friends, kind of like on Facebook.

Readers may also vote on lists of their favorite books via Listopia (more on that soon). If someone is curious about the best thriller, they can find a list for it. What is popular in cozy mysteries or naughty fiction? There's a list for it! The more votes a book receives, the higher it ranks on the list.

The best way to learn Goodreads is to sign up (goodreads.com) and explore it *from the reader perspective*. It's free to join, and figuring it out is a lot of fun. You might even discover some delightful new reads for yourself along the way.

Once you've signed up, here are some ways you can use Goodreads for marketing.

SETUP YOUR AUTHOR PAGE.

This will take an hour or two, but the investment of time is very worth it. Creating your profile is the first step to connecting with readers, just like you connect with friends on Facebook. Your author page provides statistics about your books and gives readers a place to see what you are up to and what you are reading, again, kind of like Facebook.

Once you have your profile, you can join the Goodreads Author program (https://www.goodreads.com/author/program). The Goodreads Author Program is a free feature designed to help authors reach their target audience of passionate readers. This is the perfect place for new and established authors to promote their books. Just follow the detailed instructions to complete the setup process. Being a Goodreads Author opens the door to the participation of any author in a myriad of Goodreads features. Such as …

LISTOPIA.

The Listopia (https://www.goodreads.com/list) section of Goodreads has a list of any kind of book you can imagine, and adding your books to the appropriate lists can expose you to new readers effortlessly. Simply find the lists appropriate for your books, and then choose the "add books to this list" tab. Use this opportunity to add other books similar to yours to the right lists (this is called good karma and may cause miracles). Then, ask your super fans to vote for your books.

HOST A GIVEAWAY.

Just like Amazon, Goodreads offers a terrific giveaway option. From your Author Dashboard, you can host a giveaway of your physical or digital books. I've had between 200 to over 700 people enter my giveaways (so far, I've only done physical copies). Goodreads offers giveaway statistics: on average, 750 people enter each Goodreads book giveaway. Of those, 8% will add the book to their to-read list, and 45% of the winners will review the book.

I've done giveaways for seven of my books, eighteen giveaways total. My approach to giveaways is simple: to find someone who wants my book and provide them with a copy. To help ensure they read the book, I write them a handwritten note. In the note, I thank them for requesting my book, tell them I've autographed it, and ask that if they enjoy the book to please leave an honest review. My hope is they will want to read some or all my other books, as well as find information they can use and the inspiration to use it. I like giveaways because they give me one more way to connect with readers.

Volunteer to answer questions.

Two other fantastic features on Goodreads allow you to take questions or host an entire book discussion. The Ask the Author widget allows your readers to ask you questions, as do the Q&A Discussion Groups. Each also allows readers to talk with one another about your book. Both features can help you turn readers who didn't know about your books into fans, and newfound readers into a passionate book enthusiast. Learn more here:

https://www.goodreads.com/author/featured_groups

CONNECT YOUR BLOG.

An added bonus of being a Goodreads author is the option to connect your blog directly to your profile. If you are a blogger, add your blog to your Goodreads Author Profile. Those readers just discovering you can learn more about you with little or no extra work on your part. They'll be able to see your latest blog on your Profile, click on it to read more, and even go directly to your personal website.

ASK FANS FOR REVIEWS ON GOODREADS.

Be sure to ask fans to review your books on Goodreads because it features books solely based on the number of reviews (positive or negative). When you receive an email from a reader telling you how much they love your book, in addition to asking them to leave a review at the online retailer of their choice, be sure to ask them to visit Goodreads as well (and be sure to provide a link to your Author Profile).

ASK FOR HELP.

One way to find readers is to ask for help. Post on Facebook, Twitter, or LinkedIn that you need help with: picking the title of a book, choosing between cover designs, what you should write about next, a character name, feedback as an advanced reader, or getting more reviews. Your friends want to help, and if you don't ask, you don't get!

SOCIAL MEDIA IS A GATEWAY TO FINDING READERS

While I am not the social media expert that Chris Syme is, I have learned a thing or two in my thirteen years as an indie author. To complete the picture and become a social media master, you'll want to pick up a copy of *Sell More Books with Less Social Media* and do the free companion course. It is well worth the small monetary investment and substantial time investment.

I break social media into two separate and distinct categories: social and media. I let my assistant handle the majority of my general postings, which include quotes, links to blogs, announcements about my books, or other book business messages. I focus on being social on social media. I stop by each platform once a day (or so) to interact with followers, answer questions, re-post interesting items, share cool discoveries, and connect with new people. Kevin Kruse talks about how to find time to stay on top of the various social media platforms in his book, *Text Me! Snap Me! Ask Me Anything!* He visits social media sites while his coffee is brewing in the morning. I also use "stolen moments" to check social media accounts and interact with others.

Allow me to share with you some effective
use social media to find readers:

- **Facebook.** There are three distinct ways you
  can use Facebook.

  » You most likely have a personal profile on
    Facebook. You might want to just keep that
    to friends and family. Or, like me, keeping
    in mind that nothing on the internet is
    truly private, open it up to the entire world.

  » You'll also want to create a professional
    page that highlights you as an author. This
    is where you'll do the majority of your
    posting and send the majority of people
    looking for you on Facebook. It is via your
    professional page you'll be placing ads if
    you're so inclined.

  » In addition to the above, savvy Facebookers
    start communities and invite people to
    join, creating an alliance of people who, in
    essence, can become super fans. In addition
    to my own group, The Prosperous Writers
    Mastermind, two of my favorites are The
    Miracle Morning Community and Pat's
    First Kindle Book. At first you'll be driving
    every comment, question, post, and
    discussion. Eventually, the momentum will
    take over as people feel at home and free to

share, ask questions, make posts, and offer thoughts and encouragement to others.

- **LinkedIn.** A fantastic platform for non-fiction authors (not so much for fiction authors, but you can still use some of the advice here), LinkedIn offers several options for finding readers. Increase the likelihood someone will discover your books by doing the following:

  » Add "author" and the name of your book to your work experience. Also, add your book title(s) to the Publications section and publish your articles and blog posts there as well.

  » Use a professional headshot. Make sure it's current and you look approachable.

  » Write your background summary in a conversational tone, and ensure you use keywords related to your book's topic (a.k.a. your expertise).

- **Quora.** I'm new to Quora and haven't quite found my sea legs. But at Kevin's suggestion in the aforementioned book, I hopped on and I'll find a way to include it in my daily repertoire. The reason I mention it here is because if you're a non-fiction author, Quora is quite possibly a place that is being overlooked by other non-fiction authors (just like me, until now).

- **Twitter.** On Twitter, I take Chris Syme's advice and use a pinned tweet to send people to Facebook (where I focus the majority of my social media time). You can customize your header image. Connecting with other authors on Twitter in your genre is a terrific way to make friends. Follow them, share their tweets, and recommend others follow them. Don't be surprised when others begin to do that for you.

- **Instagram.** A picture is worth a thousand *readers.* There are so many terrific ways authors can use Instagram, here are six:

  » **Follow other authors you love.** Comment on their posts, give encouragement, and be a fan.

  » **Follow bloggers who review books.** They just might decide to read and review your book!

  » **Promote your books.** I post the square image used for audiobooks on Instagram because they look so great (smile). You can post a photo on release day, to announce an upcoming release, or to host a giveaway.

» **Inspire!** Create your own images using Canva or WordSwag to inspire yourself and your followers. Use your own photo and quotes, or borrow from others (give credit where credit is due, of course).

» **Collaborate.** Join with others and use a hashtag (I love #amwriting, #authorlife, and #authorsofinstagram).

» **Share.** No need to post naked selfies or share a picture of every single meal you eat. But sharing little slices of life make you real, approachable, and *human*. So share little bits and pieces of your daily life.

• **Pinterest.** I think Pinterest is great, and whenever I need any type of recipe that's where I land. But it's also super for my author business because, just like Instagram, it is so visually oriented. With over 100 million users (and 85% of them female – also known as the gender that reads the most!), you can't ignore this platform, and used well, it can help your discoverability as an author.

» **Create a board to showcase your book covers.** You've got great covers and Pinterest is a terrific place to show them off.

» **Create a board for your blogs, too.** Whether you're sharing research for your novel, or additional tips you're discussing in your non-fiction tomes, a separate board for people to follow will increase discoverability.

» **Consider going pro.** You have the option of using a business account, which gives you insight into site analytics (but doesn't change the look of your profile to viewers). In addition, you can build authority and credibility by earning a reputation as the go-to person about a topic. Provide value and inspiration and you'll find yourself with lots of followers who can't wait to read your books.

» **Show your personality in your bio and your pins.** I believe it's our job as authors to simultaneously repel those who don't like us and attract those who do. I believe you can't do the wrong thing with the right person, and vice versa (which I discuss in my TEDx talk, *Authenticity is the New Black:* http://honoreecorder.com/authenticity-is-the-new-black/). As with all social media platforms, being yourself is the best way to find new readers. Give your readers (and future readers) a glimpse of life behind the book.

» **Install the Pin It button on your browser of choice.** Then when you see something interesting, you can pin it to the board(s) of your choosing. Those pins will show up in the timelines of your followers.

» **Ask people to follow you on Pinterest.** You can add the option to follow you on Pinterest to your blogs or email signature. You can make an ask on other social platforms.

» **Size matters.** Figure out the optimal size for your pinned images (http://pinchofyum.com/how-to-hide-an-image-in-a-wordpress-post) because longer pins with words get more re-pins than short images. If you're going to do it, you might as well do it right, right?

» **Be wordy.** You're a writer, so adding a super cool, keyword rich and inviting description of your pin isn't a stretch.

» **Stay at it.** In *The Prosperous Writer's Guide to Making More Money,* my illustrious co-author Brian suggested using a strategy long enough to know whether or not it's working. If you don't get results in 24 hours, don't be tempted to quit. Be consistent, even if you're just pinning one thing a week!

That might not be enough, but you get my gist, right?

» **Be generous and informational.** Follow and re-pin your favorite authors and resources. A single candle can light the world by first lighting other candles. Be an active candle-lighting-candle!

Notes about the above:

Use a consistent profile image so you're immediately recognizable across all platforms.

You might have noticed that some tips (ask people to follow you) apply to all platforms (but you're smart, so I knew I didn't need to repeat myself).

Check your privacy settings regularly. Be sure to use complex passwords so you won't wake up one day to find your account has been hacked. (No faster way to lose readers than to offend them or compromise their social media accounts!)

One other tip: from time to time, ask your readers how they found you. I ask in my different newsletters, in my Facebook group, and in emails I get directly from readers. Keeping track of that data can help you to figure out which of your ninja strategies are *the most ninja of all.*

LESSONS LEARNED

I learned a few lessons from asking readers where they found me, and those were:

1. Never Underestimate the Power of the Ask

Okay, this one is important, so I am repeating it. Look, if you don't a-s-k, you don't g-e-t. It's perfectly fine to get a no, but you always get a no if you don't ask in the first place! I think you'll love the book *Go for No!* by my friends Richard Fenton and Andrea Waltz. It's a good idea to let someone decide for themselves by giving them the option to buy, and along with the ask, to plant the seed that they might want to purchase the books as gifts or even premiums. Premiums are items given en masse, such as at an event in a gift bag. The order of 3,000 books for *Tall Order!* was given to attendees at the company's annual conference, conveniently held in Las Vegas (where I lived at the time). Even if you're a fiction writer, you can still ask the question!

2. Selling Direct has Multiple Advantages

First, you make and keep 100% of the profit. Second, you are a few degrees closer to the reader. *My friend/neighbor/coach wrote this book and you might like it* holds more weight than a book purchased on Amazon with no personal or emotional connection. It will most likely be read sooner, with more enthusiasm, and (I think this is super cool) the reader will lean in the direction of liking the book more than if they had discovered it on their own.

3. Front and Back Matter Can Bring Readers Closer to You

While I didn't know to put a CTA (Call to Action) in the front and back of my book (and oh, how I wish I had!), you can include something for readers to do to connect with you directly, such as download two chapters of one of your other books, or join your mailing list.

One other fantastic ninja idea.

J.A. Huss, who prolifically writes romance books, held a contest and asked her readers to change their Facebook photo to the cover image of her book. J.A. has thousands of fans, so the exposure yielded thousands of additional sales. Imagine having even

20 people change their image to the cover of your book, which their thousands of collective friends and connections would then see. Cool, right?

BRIAN'S TWO CENTS ON WHAT NOT TO DO.

Honorée is the best marketing ninja I know. I've learned a bunch from her and I want to reiterate her point about understanding that we spend money and we spend time to make our business grow.

I didn't always think this way. I had to do it wrong to learn.

In 2012, I worked at a phone center and was editing my second novel during breaks. One of the other workers was named Roy Marble. Unless you're from Iowa (or Flint, Michigan) you may not know the name. He's the all-time leading scorer for the University of Iowa men's basketball team and played on the legendary team that went 30–5 in the late eighties. They won their first eighteen games of the season and made it to number one in the nation.

We started talking and he was interested in hearing about my book business. I saw this as a sign he might want a writer to collaborate on a book about him and the Iowa Hawkeye team that did so well.

I was right, and it led to me writing his story about that season. Roy got the university to allow us to launch the book at the Penn State game where 20,000 people would be cheering on their favorite team in Black and Gold. How many authors get a chance to launch like that?

WE SOLD A BUNCH OF BOOKS.

It seemed reasonable to keep pushing the sales by setting up some signings. We did a few in Iowa City and other cities close to the university and then reached out to a major grocery store chain. I arranged to have Roy and me do a signing at each of thirty stores in the greater Des Moines area over three weekends.

The grocery store chain included the times and dates for our signing in their email blast and print advertisement the week before we arrived and it did a great job of getting people to come in and meet the author … okay, nobody wanted to meet me, but they did get a thrill out of meeting Roy.

When all was said and done, we sold around 800 copies. When I got done giving Roy his share, paying for the books, the gas, the food, and everything else. I made just over $200.00

It was an exhausting lesson in ROTI.

There are several things to take away from this story.

1. Getting people to buy from you directly can give one more margin, but it can also lead to greater expenses. So, the margin may not be as good as you think at first.

2. All those sales don't get "recorded" anywhere. They don't improve the ranking of the book on Amazon and this means we don't get additional sales from organic traffic.

3. Doing a book signing is fun ... the first couple of times. Then it becomes something you'd rather avoid. The people are nice and it's flattering to scrawl your name across the book, but it doesn't take long before the chit-chat becomes so repetitive that it's hard to keep one's enthusiasm. I was really burned out on signings before we even did the first one in the series of thirty because we had already done five or six others. Yes, it only took five or six for the thrill of the book signing to wear off.

The moral of this story is that one can be a better marketing ninja by deciding NOT to do some things.

ONE MORE NINJA THING

Honorée is even more of a ninja master than she knows. Not only does she come up with these brilliant ideas for marketing, but she also shares them, and has taught me how to think like a marketing assassin.

I've implemented her strategies recently and now it's part of my mindset. I'm constantly on the lookout for opportunities to leave a card or book, and it's got me thinking like a ninja.

Ninja marketing is fun and I want to do more. (I hope you do, too!)

I'm working on adding two pages to each of my print versions and ordering new copies just for leaving in coffee shops and tiny libraries. The page will simply read, "I'm a Travelling Book ... When you're done, leave me someplace else (but don't forget to put a comment about where you found me below)" and then have two pages where people can write about how they found the book.

One can imagine a person finding the book and being just as intrigued by where it's been as the actual story. I'm sure the "Travel Pages" will be just as much a hook as the story.

How fun would it be to discover one of your books after it had been roaming around the world for a couple of years? That's my own ninja idea. But it's because Honorée has got me thinking outside the box that I came up with it.

THINK LIKE A NINJA

Honorée again. I love what Brian said about thinking like a ninja, because that is exactly what I have in mind for you, the reader! I didn't originate thinking like a ninja; I learned it from other ninjas who were doing things I hadn't thought of until I heard their ideas. I believe you can take any idea you hear and improve upon it. Claudia Azula Altucher wrote a great book called *Become an Idea Machine*, which you should totally pick up and devour. In her book, she encourages her readers to brainstorm ten new ideas a day. New ideas for anything and everything that's important to you, captured in your journal, can and will spark other ideas. One of them is bound to inspire you or even make you a fortune. Imagine brainstorming ten new book marketing ideas a day, using the ones we've shared in this book? Of course, they won't all be home runs, but if even one of your ideas works wonders, won't you be stoked?

Okay, now that you have a pretty long list of ways to find readers, I'm going to turn it over to Brian, who is going to walk you through some additional lessons he's learned along the way. You'll love not only learning about his journey, but also finding even more gems of inspiration in this next section.

SECTION THREE

CHART YOUR JOURNEY

BRIAN HERE.

I thought I'd take some time to tell you some of the things I've learned along the way. Not everything worked as I had hoped.

When I began, my plan was to build a blog following and then I wanted to bundle my blog posts into a book and sell it. I had been getting a few readers with my snarky woodworking blog that had daily posts chronicling my success and many failures. The reasoning in my mind was that if people enjoyed my humor in little daily posts, they would surely like a collection of those posts.

The first day of blogging happened quite by accident. I came upon a site called Blogger while bored and wrote a post about my foibles in cutting the legs to my workbench. Apparently, measure twice and cut once, which I did, still doesn't get the job done if one is measuring while watching college football.

I had legs of three different lengths and the two that matched were wrong.

After my first blog post, I found a forum on woodworking called Lumberjocks.com. An hour of exploration later and I joined. While setting up the details for my account, I noticed that one could blog on the site. I had already blogged!

Back to Blogger I went. A quick copy and paste later the post was in both places. It felt productive and despite my pure, white-hot hatred of writing, I had enjoyed my little self-mocking rant.

It should be mentioned that this was Jan 2, 2010. I was almost 44 years old and had hated writing since eighth grade. My degree is in economics from Iowa State University. I've yet to take my first writing course.

The mindset on that first day was that I was bored and this little post was simply me entertaining myself. At that point, there wasn't any thought of blogging regularly or one day writing a novel. Those things just never occurred to me.

It's funny how one's perceptions can change with a little (or a lot) of external validation.

On Jan 3, 2010, I woke up and returned to Lumberjocks to read more woodworking stories before heading to the lumberyard to buy more 4x4s to replace the legs I'd made too short. I was shocked.

The little post I'd put up without much thought had been read over 300 times and there were 25 comments. These other woodworkers loved my humor. They told me they had laughed and that my mistakes were ones they'd all made, too, so I shouldn't get discouraged. Mostly they said they wanted more.

I had readers!

The end.

Okay, that wasn't the end. In fact, it turned out to be much harder to convert those readers into book buying customers, or even into blog followers.

At that time in my life, I was living below the poverty line. My parents had let me reside in my grandfather's place, so there was a roof over my head. I had a part-time job doing some social media stuff for a tiny start-up in DC. It was just enough to buy food and pay the utilities.

I was happy, but the thought of making a little extra money was on my mind. So, I wrote another post on Jan 3. I kept writing and getting lots of readers on Lumberjocks. Many of them read every day and left comments.

The plan was to set up my own blog. I figured after a month or so, which would give me time to figure out HOW to set up a blog, I'd tell the Lumberjocks readers and they'd tune in each day.

Well, it didn't work like that. Once I had ExtremelyAverage.com running with daily posts (and the other posts I'd previous written), the folks on Lumberjocks mostly wanted to get my daily updates the way they'd always gotten them before.

My blog numbers were sad.

Eventually, I explained that I was going to only be posting on my blog. Most of the readers didn't follow. I learned that many people are skeptical by nature. They feared that I might be trying to build a business that could make me money. I was doing just that. I like money (and the food that it buys).

Undaunted and knowing I was basically back to square one, I kept at it. When you're at the bottom, there's little reason not to keep going. In fact, Daymond John, the founder and CEO of FUBU, wrote a book called *The Power of Broke*. I just read it and wish it had been around in 2010, because his ideas are sound and motivational. I needed some of that. All I had was a literal hunger for more ... pizza and Chinese food.

Something interesting happened as I was writing my blog every day. I was always looking for new and creative ways to craft a post and one day the decision was made to do the post as a chapter of a mystery novel.

I hadn't done any woodworking that day. In fact, all I'd done was buy a Bosch 1.25 HP router. I'd been saving up and talking about it all month on the blog, so the few readers I had knew it was in the cards. A noir mystery starring a detective who liked woodworking and the Brooklyn Dodgers would be perfect.

I named my P.I. Henry Wood.

Henry Wood lived in Brooklyn and had a small agency in Manhattan. In his Brooklyn house, there was a strange closet that occasionally sent him things from the future. He didn't understand it, but liked the last present he'd been given, a Bosch router.

Yes, my detective story had a time travel closet. It was the only way I could figure out to work in the "clue" that I'd finally bought the router. It didn't matter that it was an incongruous thing to have in an historical detective story if one was never going to finish the story.

My readers loved it.

I've written four complete Henry Wood novels and am working on the fifth. There have been more than a few reviews where people sort of shook their head at the closet, but there have also been those who love it. In hindsight, I do think that the silly closet has cost me readers, but that's okay; that closet started me on a path that changed my life.

STAGES OF THE JOURNEY

After a couple of years without much of an idea of where I wanted to go, I realized it was crucial to visualize the signposts on my journey. The following five stages are what I charted out for my book business. The first four might be good for anyone, but the fifth, that's where you'll want to craft your own ultimate destination.

Goals are important. This is something that both Honorée and I agree on 100%. It's best to write them down. I didn't always do that, and I'm sure it slowed my progress, but I did think about them all the time. Now, I keep an Excel file and a notebook where I do write the goals and ideas down.

When I was starting out, I just wanted to make one thousand dollars per month from my writing. If I could do that, it would make my life much easier.

When I quit my day job in late 2015, I had had three months in a row that were all well beyond my goal: $3,000, $7,000, and then $9,800. I left my job and never looked back. There have been a lot of five-figure months since then. Not all of them, though, sometimes sales drop because there's a change in how people react to one's marketing. Then, one needs to regroup and tweak things.

But this is not what we're here to talk about. We want to show people how they build their initial readers and get from zero to one thousand, and once there, where they might want to set their sights.

So, back when my best month ever was $600, I thought about what it had taken to get there and I decided that this mark was Stage One for me.

STAGE ONE

This is when one has only one or two books and if the author isn't telling people about the books, they simply don't sell. It's when the books have fewer than ten reviews.

It's the beginning.

My nature is that I'm an outgoing person who enjoys mingling with others. It isn't hard for me to strike up conversations. I enjoy selling and from a young age found I had a knack for it.

When I was ten, my hockey team in Ames, Iowa, was raising funds. Did we sell cookies? No. We sold the much sexier product, lawn fertilizer. Feel free to insert joke here.

I still remember that the makeup of the fertilizer was 20-10-10, which was supposed to be good. I canvassed the neighborhood and rang every doorbell. Everyone had a lawn and I had a solution to their lawn care needs. Being ten, I think I got most of my sales because I was freaking adorable with my confident pitch.

There was a contest to see who could sell the most bags. I won going away.

The next year, though, it wasn't my pitch that did the job, it was the product because everyone saw great results. I went back and asked for repeat orders and everyone bought again. I thought I was a great salesman. I won the contest a second time.

Sales is about confidence and I probably wasn't a great pitchman at ten or eleven, but the cute of the first year and the repeat sales of the second year gave me a false sense that I was closing the deal. It stuck with me.

Confidence has never been a problem.

So, asking someone for a review, that's about the easiest pitch ever. I truly love my books. No problem, right?

For the first couple of years, I hated it. Asking for a review made my stomach turn. It caused all sorts of stress. It wasn't that I feared a negative review or anything of the sort, it just seemed like the most horrible thing to bother people I liked with and that it would eat up, at the very least, hundreds of hours of their time, probably causing a rift in their marriage, leading to divorce, and lifelong psychological problems for their children. It was quite a burden to carry.

Writing a review takes very little time. Most people are happy to help. The ones that don't want to do it will blow it off. No friendships are harmed in the process and the most important part is that it works.

I had to get over my fear of asking. It's the second most important things one can do when starting out. The first is setting up your mailing list, but we'll talk about that later.

I'm sure there are people out there who never have "review request phobia" and that's awesome. For those of us who do, it's important to ask anyway.

I knew that my fear of failing as an author was greater than the uncomfortable moment when I'd say, *Hey, thanks for letting me know you read my book. Would you mind popping onto Amazon and leaving a review?*

In Stage One we must get reviews, and the focus needs to be on getting to ten. It's harder to go from zero to ten than it is to go from 100 to 200 because of the numbers of sales one needs to get a single review organically. Often it can take one hundred sales to get a single review without asking.

When you've just published your first book, getting to 1,000 sales, so that you can have ten reviews, is almost impossible unless you already have the ten reviews to get people to buy your book. It's a vicious oval. (Circle is so overused in this instance.)

The smaller sites, which are where everyone should start, often require eight to ten reviews, such as Ereader News Today and BKNights.

So, those first ten need to be rounded up. You'll need to beg friends and family. Yes, those reviews will be biased and tend to be five stars.

FINDING THE RIGHT READERS & REVIEWERS

HONORÉE HERE.

I've put together advanced reader teams for the last dozen or so of my books, as well as for the books in *The Miracle Morning* book series. In addition to my personal experience, I have learned from super secret sources I cannot name here, as well as hearing Bryan Cohen and Jim Kukral (the co-hosts of the Sell More Books Show) and Chris Fox, author of *Six-Figure Author*, as they've talked about how to get reviews. In addition, you don't just want reviews, you want the *right reviews.* Allow me to explain.

Reviews, specifically verified reviews (a review by someone who is confirmed to have purchased the book), left by the avatar for your book help Amazon's algorithms to market the book to other people (lots of other people!). This is done by identifying common characteristics of those who have reviewed the book. With as few as ten reviews, the ideal reader can be identified for your book. Then, Amazon can begin marketing the book aggressively and specifically to others who fit the same profile: those with a high likelihood to buy, read, and love it.

When this step is overlooked or not followed exactly, you miss the short-term and, most importantly, long-term opportunity to have Amazon work on your behalf to promote the book. Most people don't realize this and think any one review is as good as the next or any verified review is a great idea. As you can see, this is not the case.

How do you find them?

If you're a non-fiction author, you should have direct access to your target avatar (ideal reader) because you are an expert in your field. Do your best to find a dozen or more of your clients or connections who have an interest, and ask them to buy (even if you provide a free copy), read, and review your book.

I have, in the past, offered to reimburse readers the cost of the purchase of the book. To date, no-one has taken me up on that offer.

Fiction authors must find readers who already enjoy books in their particular genre. For example, I'm working on a series of thrillers. I'm looking for a few dozen people to read and review my first three books when they are ready. (If this is you, go here to join my fiction Advanced Reader Team at HonoreeCorder.com/HCCorder). I advise you ask anyone and everyone if they read and love the type of books you write. Offer to provide a copy in exchange for an honest review. Because online retailers track the data and profiles of those who leave reviews, it won't be long before they will be marketing your book to people you might not otherwise be able to reach—just because they share a similar love of your type of book.

Make sense? Okay, I'll pass the baton back to Brian.

Brian again.

Yes, most readers will know that a book with only a handful of reviews isn't really a 4.9 average. Those readers will still be willing to click on "Look Inside" and perhaps it will be worth their while.

One of the key elements in driving sales is running promotions where one gives one's book away for free or puts it on sale for ninety-nine cents. Honorée talked about this some and she's right. There are many venues that will accept your ads, but the best ones have guidelines in regard to the number of reviews the book must have before it's eligible for promotion.

This is especially true of books that are free or ninety-nine cents.

In Stage One you want to go after every review you can imagine.

A word of caution, though, is don't try to game the system with fake reviews. Amazon, in particular, is clever. They will catch those reviews and hit the delete button. In fact, there have been so many people trying to cheat that Amazon tends to err on the side of delete. This may one day cause a legitimate review to disappear and that can be frustrating. Don't blame Amazon, blame the authors who are trying to take a shortcut.

Please remember that it takes years of hard work to become an overnight success. (Honorée's note: Amen.) Also, if writing is something you enjoy, then worrying about how quickly you make it to your goal is silly. You're having fun along the way and when the day comes that you can do it full-time (if that's your goal), it will be a nice moment, but it isn't the only goal. First and foremost, writing should be about exploring what you can do as a writer and taking pride in the progress that comes with the journey.

The short version is this ...

1. Ask people to review your book.

2. Always be asking so that it is part of your routine. That means that if someone asks about your book, you tell them, and they say they may check it out, go ahead and ask them if they could please write a review afterward. Do it even if you think they are just being nice. Who knows, they may buy your book and do exactly as they said.

3. Use the smaller sites that don't require eight to ten reviews to run promotions. Any time you get your book into someone's hands, you've done a good thing for your business.

4. Be honest (leave the cheating for the cheaters). Work hard and you'll find it's worth it.

Stage Two

There is one site that is better than all the rest. It's called BookBub and that's where you want to advertise your book.

Sounds easy, right?

No.

Everyone wants to advertise their books on BookBub because the results are amazing, but there are a limited number of slots available each day, so placement is competitive. I've had free promotions that included a BookBub promotion and the difference between them and other venues can be 40,000 downloads versus 3,000.

In every promotion I've had through them, currently at thirteen, my ROI (return on investment) has been at least 500% and usually an additional 50–130 reviews.

The more reviews your book has, the better the chance someone will buy it. Of course, there are some people who don't care about review totals. Maybe you're one of those people. Maybe you think the reviews are all biased. You are not representative of the reading population.

If you can remind yourself daily, *I am not my reader*, it will serve you well. One mistake I've made repeatedly is that without any data to support my decisions, I assume the way I think about books is universal (or at the very least in the majority).

This is dangerous because it can cause one to miss countless opportunities.

The biggest example in my life of how this type of thinking has cost me thousands of dollars is the idea (in my mind) that nobody reads paper books anymore. I read 98% of the books I buy on my iPad or iPhone, so I assume everyone does the same. This idea was so strong in my mind that I've not bothered to make print versions available for most of my books. Even now, only half of them have print versions, which is something I'm working on fixing.

You know what happened when I started putting up my print books for sale? Some people bought them. My Kindle sales are still the biggest part of my monthly revenue, but the percentage is shifting. Six months ago, when I only had two of twelve titles in print, less than one tenth of one percent of my sales were print.

I used this ridiculous statistic to justify *not* putting my books into InDesign and getting the layout done so I could sell the print versions. *Print just doesn't sell for fiction,* my voice would say.

The little voice in my head should have been yelling, *How do you know?! You don't even give readers the chance to buy the paper version.*

Even after people would email me asking when the paperback would be available, I still resisted.

My last month revenue saw print making up 2.3%, which was up from the month before and has grown every month over the last few since I started making them available. I spend a ton of money on advertising and now the people that prefer the print version have that as an option.

This is why we don't assume we are our reader. I've left thousands, perhaps tens of thousands of dollars on the table over the last few years. What's worse, and this is nearly unforgivable, I've left potential avid fans on the table.

This book is about finding your true fans because they're the key to success. They're the ones who will buy everything you put out. If you get enough of these fine folks, you'll be able to do this for a living.

So, back to my point about the importance of reviews. If we think like a statistician, then we need to consider the entire book-buying population. If there is a pool of, say, ten million readers, we know that some of them read mystery books. Let's say we're talking about four million people. Of those people, their buying habits will vary. Some will buy only e-books, others will only check out books from the library, others prefer print, while some want used books bought in cozy indie bookstores with cats on staff.

This means that the reasons one buys a book can be just as varied. Some people will judge a book by its cover. Others will read the description and that will be the key to their decisions. Some will use the "Look Inside" feature and go from there. A portion will begin with the number of reviews and the rating. I would wager that every person has a habit they stick to. In each case, there will be a first step.

If that first step is deciding if the cover is appealing, then you'd better have a good cover. If it is social proof, then you better have reviews.

All of this is to say that the monetary ROI is only part of the picture, and getting a bunch more reviews from a BookBub promotion is more valuable than you may imagine.

Stage Two involves getting enough reviews to give yourself the best chance of being chosen for one of those coveted BookBub slots. They are picky. In their rejection notice, which most people will get on their first try, the email states that they reject 80% of the submissions. (Note: Not my wonderful co-author, Honorée, though. She was one for one out the gate.)

The reasons for rejections are many. Poor cover design, weak book descriptions on the sales pages of the various sites (such as Amazon, Barnes & Noble, Kobo, Apple iBooks, and Google Play), and just sheer volume of submissions can all play a part.

We know from statements made publicly by BookBub representatives that they don't have a specific minimum guideline for number of reviews, but they have said that they like to see fifty.

Yes, the big Five-Oh is your goal for Stage Two. You want to get your first BookBub ad and add a bunch of juice to your sales.

There's one other aspect of the BookBub promotions that is probably the most valuable over the lifetime of your career. It's that you pick up extra subscribers to your mailing list. Again, we'll talk about that later.

So, you've managed to get to ten reviews in Stage One. Now, in Stage Two, you're still thinking about garnering reviews while you work on your next book. The venues that require eight to ten reviews are available and you're using them to promote your book.

Run promotions and keep at it until you hit fifty.

It doesn't hurt to start submitting to BookBub in Stage Two. You may sneak in with fewer than fifty and that will launch you into Stage Three. Just be prepared. Each rejection stings a little. It's the same with one-star reviews. You'll need to build a coping mechanism for those tiny gut punches. We all go through it. In fact, pick one of your favorite authors and go read her one-star reviews.

STAGE THREE

For me I felt I'd reached a third stage when I was consistently getting BookBub advertisements at a pace of four or five per year. Once I knew what it took and that no matter how cool I thought I was, I would still get rejected most of the time, I stopped worrying about it.

One trick I found that has worked for me is to put in for an ad at ninety-nine cents and then if it gets rejected, immediately come back with a request for a

FREE promotion. This strategy helped me get more BookBub ads and improved my bottom line.

Most of my ads have been for FREE promotions and the results are always profitable and help build readership.

Realizing that I would need to do more than just BookBub ads to continue the growth, I started looking to venues like Facebook, Instagram, and Amazon for advertising.

These methods of advertising are more of a challenge. One needs to do a fair amount of study to figure out what works.

I started out by taking a course on Facebook Ads and it failed for me. The course was well-designed and I liked the teachers. The information was helpful because I learned enough to be able to place ads, but their target audience was people who were selling much larger ticket items like consulting. At the end of the course, the teacher even said he didn't know how one could use Facebook for selling books because the margin was so small.

The next one I took was Mark Dawson's Facebook Advertising for Authors Course. It's designed for authors and made all the difference in the world. Still, it's a great challenge to do profitably and you will need to understand that most of the things you try will fail. You must test and test and test to find a plan that works. It requires a lot of time and patience.

I've had similar experiences with all the places I've looked into advertising on a cost-per-click basis. Each one has challenges.

The upside is that once you crack one of these platforms, your revenue goes up substantially. Depending upon the month, I might spend $2,000–$4,000 on advertising and will typically get an ROI of 100%–300%.

Please understand that ROI isn't the only important measure, and sometimes I'd rather have lower ROI with a higher actual profit left over at the end of the month. As an example, I had two months last year where the ROI was vastly different, but the lower one was preferable.

In Month One I spent $4,000 on ads, and in Month Two I spent $700.

———

In Month One, I had a profit of $7,800, while my Month Two profit was only $5,300. So while my ROI for Month Two was the greatest (757%), it was actually Month One where I made the most money, even though my ROI was much less (195%).

———

One might ask the question, "Why didn't you spend the $4,000 in Month Two and really crush it?"

I would have if it had been possible. The hardest part about the various advertising platforms is figuring out how and when to scale. Some months the clicks are cheap, while others they are expensive. I spend as much as I can and keep an eye on which ads are performing well.

In the case of the second month, I had a couple ads that were crushing it. I tried to create similar ads to scale up the spend, but those ads just didn't do well.

In the first month, I had lots of ads performing reasonably well and could spend a lot more money, even though it was at a lower ROI.

The point is to have as much money left over at the end of the month. This profit or throughput is the ultimate goal, so some advertising decisions require looking at the big picture and making the decisions accordingly. If I had tried to spend $4,000 in the second month, most of those ads would have lost money and I wouldn't have been left with $5,300. It would have been much less.

In this stage, which is where I consider myself now, one can expect a lot of months with five-figure sales (summer months can be a challenge). The more of those months one has, the larger one's reader base becomes.

To do well in this business, you'll need to keep writing and producing new work or eventually the sales will dry up. The further through each stage you get, the longer the tail becomes on how quickly sales drop when you take a break.

In my above ROI example, a portion of those sales would have happened regardless. In my internal calculations, I factor in the read through and existing reader base to get a less inflated number.

To better understand how much of my revenue was being driven from ad sales, I took the month of July 2016 off from running ads. When I last did this in 2013, my sales went from $400-600 a month down to $150.

This time the sales dropped to $3,000. I then ramped up my advertising again and was able to get back to five-figures almost immediately. I know it seems crazy to give up so much revenue, but I truly value the data. Also, the month of July was such that I didn't really have the time to manage my ads like I typically would, so it was a perfect time for a test.

This example is just to reinforce the power of working your way through the stages. I'm confident that my sales will continue be enough to support being a full-time author even through dry spells of writing. It means that if I want to take a vacation, I don't stress out about it. Even a break can be profitable if it gets one's writing juices replenished.

Stage Four

It's important to remember that my five stages are simply a construct I've created to allow me to keep focused. It may be wise to plan your own stages based upon your objectives. I'm sure it would serve you better than simply adopting mine, but I hope it gives you a sense for the theme of stages.

I've been a full-time author for over a year. Financially, I'm doing better than I have ever done before, so it begs the question, why even have other stages?

I don't *need* to make more money. I do have a burning desire to pursue other projects and dreams, though. I keep a journal of ideas that I'd like to go after. They range from wanting to buy a manufacturing company, to starting an alternative energy company, to inventing new technology that improves upon existing tech. I dream big.

Most of these ideas will require money. So, to continue to grow and explore my passions, I give you Stage Four.

This is the point where I focus on building a strong enough list to be able to launch books onto *The New York Times Best Sellers* list.

I've never been on *The New York Times* or *USA Today* lists. I'm less interested in the moniker "*The New York Times* bestselling author or *USA Today* bestselling author" than I am cracking the math behind doing it on a consistent basis. It isn't complex. Just grow a big list of avid readers.

Let's assume that most weeks one can crack the *USA Today* list for fiction with 10,000 sales in a week (usually, I have 2,000–3,000 sales over an entire month). It's a big number to be sure.

Working the math backward, let's start with 10,000 and divide that by point two. Go ahead and punch that into the calculator on your phone. It gives you the number 50,000. That's the number of people that need to open your email blast at a rate of 20% click through, to get the 10,000 people to your page for the new book.

But it's not that simple. Not all of those people will buy it.

So, let's say we know that 1 in 3 of your fans who click will buy it, then you need 150,000 people to open your email.

How many people on an email list would it take to get 150,000 to open it?

I've talked with many authors and most of them find that 50–60% open rate is reasonable. This is *much* better than the industry standard for newsletters, which is 12.5%. And the click through rate for authors is typically 20–22%.

That means that a 300,000 people list would probably do the trick. It may be a smaller number depending upon how one manages one's list. If one sends regular messages, that could mean a higher open average. If one has a series where people are dying for the next installment, it may not require a list of even half that size.

There are lots of variables, but that's what Stage Four is all about. Building the list, testing the results, trying to improve the results, and then using it as a tool to achieve one's goals.

Another factor with my example of trying to launch on a list is that one may also be doing targeted ads or have run a quality pre-order campaign.

All the sales during the time your book is up for pre-order count in that first week. So, if you can convince 2,000 people to pre-order, then the target is easier to hit.

The point is that a mailing list of substantial size can vault your titles into a whole other level of exposure. Getting enough sales in one week to make a list will also land your book near the top of Amazon's Overall Top Seller list, which is more exposure.

Perhaps your list is only good enough to get you 7,000 sales, but you get them all on a Monday or Tuesday and the book is on page one of the Top 100 for a couple of days and is #1 across your sub categories. That will yield more sales.

For me, this stage is all about scaling up in a much bigger way than I've done through Stage Three.

STAGE FIVE

I'll be the first to admit that when I first imagined Stage Five, it was the sort of dream that one puts out there, a seemingly unachievable goal. It still feels that way, but I find value in having it there, waiting for me. Perhaps when I get deep into Stage Four, I can give it some serious thought.

My Stage Five is selling one of my novels as a movie. I had imagined that I'd write a screenplay for *Killing Hemingway* and I still might, but I've since learned that most studios prefer that the author *not* write the screenplay. They would rather have an A-List Screenwriter, A-List Producer, and A-List Director so that if it goes poorly, they don't get blamed since they had all the right people. I get that.

Still, I would like to learn the craft of screenplay writing, so I may use *Killing Hemingway* to try it out.

My Stage Five is unlikely to be anyone else's Stage Five, especially if you are a non-fiction writer, but that's okay. It's a great idea to make your own stages (or at the very least, this last one).

When the day comes that I have achieved this goal, I'll likely create five more stages to help guide me from that point in my life. What's important is to have a plan, something you can visualize daily, which will help as a guide through decision making. Each day your hours are limited and right now you're focused on gaining readers. Once you get good at picking up some loyal fans, you don't want to get stagnant; that's why having a few milestones well off in the distance will keep you from periods of being unproductive.

GROWING YOUR MAILING LIST

Not growing my mailing list is something I did horribly wrong for the first few years of my business. I'm just now understanding the power of the list and where I went wrong.

When I began, I had my blog and people could subscribe. Every time another author would give advice about the importance of "your list," I thought that they meant my list of subscribers. A strong blog subscriber list is a wonderful thing but it is *not* the same as an author list. People who enjoy daily posts of 500–1,000 words may not be interested in your books. They may not want to hear about your new release. Of course, you'll certainly mention the new tome on the blog and it will drive some sales, but it isn't the same as a dedicated list.

The author newsletter is an important tool. And there are things you must understand about it to fully appreciate the necessity of dedicating time to the building of such a list.

As I mentioned above but is worth repeating, the following three points are crucial to know.

1. Never call it a newsletter. I suggest, instead, calling it an "author reader group."

2. Typical newsletters have an open rate of 12.5%. Author reader groups open their emails at a rate of 50–60%.

3. CTR (click-thru rates) for newsletters is 1–2%, while author reader groups click through 20% of the time.

4. The reason one never calls their newsletter a newsletter is because that term has been beaten to death and people are tired of getting newsletters. Avid readers, however, love hearing from their favorite authors. Being part of a reader group seems much less intrusive.

I learned this from Nick Stephenson and Mark Dawson, both of whom tested landing page copy using "newsletter" versus "reader group" and the results were clear. I've also done my own tests and my results were similar to what they had found. People are 50% more likely to sign up for your list if it is a reader group than if they're asked to subscribe to a newsletter.

There may come a day where "reader group" is beaten to death and at that point we'll need to come up with another idea, but until then, use READER GROUP.

The reason it's handy to remember the open and click-thru rates is that those benchmarks will aid in guiding you as you write your emails that go out to the readers.

STYLE AND COPY MATTER

When I worked as a data analyst in the marketing department at a major insurance company, I learned that they always tested their advertising mailing envelopes to see which design performed the best. The control group would be a plain white envelope and there would usually be four to six designs created by the art department. It is interesting to note that during my five years in that department, the control group (blank white) never lost. At the time, I believe it was undefeated. For some reason, those blank envelopes were opened more often (we surmised the open rate because the material inside was the same across all the envelopes and included unique telephone numbers that allowed tracking) but that didn't stop the art department from continuing to look for a way to improve.

Remember this story when you're testing your own emails. Try some fancy ones with lots of pretty pictures and designs for part of your list. Then do a plain "get to the point" email with minimal design and see which one wins.

(Honorée here: I've tried fancy and simple. Simple wins every time.)

You'll learn a lot about your audience that way.

It isn't just the design you should test. My own experience has been that the copywriting is incredibly important. In fact, I'd recommend taking the time to read a book or two on the subject (*The AdWeek Copywriting Handbook: The Ultimate Guide to Writing Powerful Advertising and Marketing Copy from One of America's Top Copywriters* by Joseph Sugarman is my favorite). Copywriting is an art form. This is especially true in emails.

You're not just picking the right words, you're also making decisions regarding the length of paragraphs. Hint: Short and sweet is the way to go.

It was hard for me to switch gears from writing prose to writing copy. For a long time, I assumed that because my readers liked my writing style, I should stick to that for my emails. I assumed incorrectly. My readers want the facts.

They want me to get to the point.

Do some tests and find out what your readers want.

Not to dwell on the whole "read some ad copy books" thing, but once I understood the goals and methods of great copywriters, it changed how I created my ads. More importantly, it changed how I viewed the description I wrote for the books on my Amazon pages.

Before reading about ad copy, there were few things in the world I hated more than writing that 200–300 word description. Those things were peas, fruit in Jell-O, and my inability to dunk (I'm short).

Once I had learned a few tips and tricks, I tried reworking my book descriptions and found that the next day my sales conversions went up. I was running the same number of ads. They were getting the typical number of clicks but those clicks were resulting in more paid sales and KU downloads (as judged by a spike the following day in page reads)

Having copywriting skills will help with your reader group emails, your description, and the way you write when trying to persuade someone that you're the right person for the job. Let me explain the last one.

There's a great thing called HARO, which stands for Help a Reporter Out. It's a three-time daily email blast that all authors should subscribe to because of the opportunities it can provide. Each email contains calls for experts in various areas to be interviewed for articles, blogs, and podcasts. The reporters put out these calls and then people write them back. If your response piques their interest, it may lead to your story getting included in their article or them asking you to be interviewed for a podcast or show.

For the first two years I subscribed, I didn't have a single one of my responses hit the mark. Once I started using what I'd learned about copywriting, I was able to craft emails that kept the reporter reading. That's the key. The first line needs to be short and intriguing enough that they want to read the second line. It's about moving the reader through your message all the way until the end.

When I get to the end, then I bust out my author skills and create a cliff hanger sort of call to action. The action being, "If you want to hear the rest of the story, I'd be happy to talk to you."

It isn't just blogs, podcasts, and newspapers that are looking for people to interview. I just opened the HARO from last night and Fox News Network, Online Wall Street Journal, CNBC, and the Associated Press (AP) all were searching for experts. It takes only a couple of minutes per day to scan the request emails and see if there's anything with which you might be able to help.

Here's an example of one I wrote to a podcast looking for marketing people who had overcome a PR nightmare.

> Dear Rob (not his real name),
>
> I'm a full-time author who almost destroyed my career with one tiny blunder at 3:00 a.m.
>
> In the world of indie publishing (and now traditional, too) the most coveted advertising spot is a listing in the daily email blasts of BookBub. They are the king makers.
>
> I had secured a spot for the fourth mystery in my *Henry Wood Detective* series, *Edge of Understanding,* and was so thrilled I couldn't sleep the night before the promotion. It would become the best day of my life ... for ten minutes before disaster struck.
>
> Typically, a BookBub ad will also give a small boost to an author's other books. *Henry Wood: Edge of Understanding* was going to be FREE for two days. I'd had other similar promotions for the first three books in the series and each time they had risen to the #3 spot on the overall Top 100 Amazon free rankings. This was the highest rated of my four books with 4.6/5 stars on 50+ reviews and it was my best cover.

This would be the time I finally made it to number one!

The email blast went out at 10:00 a.m. and the downloads started pouring in at a rate of around 190 per minute for the first hour. I was refreshing my report page so fast there was a risk of serious finger injury.

When four o'clock rolled around, I checked and my book had hit #1. I was so excited I literally jumped around a bit. It was a goal reached and I couldn't be more thrilled.

Ten minutes later there was a new review. One-star. The person was not happy with the book they received. I shrugged. It happens. A few minutes later there was another one-star review and the person was complaining that *Henry Wood* wasn't even in book four.

What?

I went to Amazon and checked the "Look Inside."

My heart sank. The world stopped turning for a moment. I knew what had happened.

My satire, *Underwood, Scotch, and Wry*, had just been released. At 3:00 a.m. I received an email with the mention of a single typo that had been found. The beauty of being both author and publisher was that it took me only a few seconds to fix and then to recompile it.

The problem was that I was tired. I got onto my dashboard and uploaded the fixed version of *Underwood, Scotch, and Wry* but not over the old version. I uploaded over *Edge of Understanding*.

At the point where I realized what I had done, 40,000 copies of the WRONG book had been sent out. People were pissed. They were leaving one-star reviews at an alarming pace.

There were tears as I sat at my desk watching my best book's review rating plummet to 3.2. My first thought was that I'd destroyed one of my novels that I'd worked so hard on. At the time, it was a big chunk of my monthly revenue, too, so that made it even more dire.

And my #1 ranking was now a source of pain not joy.

If you'd like to hear the rest of the story and learn how I turned the worst day of my life into a positive, please let me know.

Sincerely,

Brian D Meeks (Sometimes Arthur Byrne)

Let's look at that email. I started with a hook. In most copy, I try to keep the hook short because the reader may not give it a chance if it looks too long, but I figured Rob was seeking people to interview for his podcast, so he would at least read the first sentence.

In the first sentence, I told him what I do and hinted at a disaster that I had to overcome. There was also a bit of a hook in the time of 3:00 a.m. It adds a bit of mystery.

What could I possibly have been doing at that hour that could ruin my career?

Then I went into storytelling mode and laid out the details of my horrible blunder.

I finish the story, talking about how much pain it caused me to think about reaching number one. I've told this story to people enough (and it's 100% true) to know that by the time I get to the end, they feel sick for me. Some probably feel almost as bad as I did at the time. Most people can remember a time they did something completely by accident and messed something up. It resonates.

But here is where my understanding of copywriting paid off. I didn't tell Rob what I did next. In the beginning, I hint at the fact that the blunder only "almost" destroyed my career.

I finish with a call to action. If Rob wants to hear the happy ending to the story, he'll have to reach out to me and continue the conversation.

He did just that and I was interviewed for his podcast. It went extremely well.

GET MORE CONVERSIONS

Now that you're convinced of the importance of building your reader group, you need to understand the importance of what Nick Stephenson describes as "reader magnets" in his excellent book: *Reader Magnets: Build Your Author Platform and Sell more Books on Kindle.* In short, a reader magnet is something of value that you give away to help close the deal on the potential reader signing up for your reader group. Honorée sometimes uses the first two chapters of her books, other times she gives away valuable resources useful to her readers.

The most common way to do this in fiction is to give away the first book of a series. I do this for my mystery, science fiction, and satire series. I know that if I can get people to take the first book in these series that they are more than likely to buy the next book and possibly continue reading until the end of the series. Furthermore, some of those readers will enjoy my writing enough that they will jump to another one of my series.

The beauty of the age in which we live is that our books are a zero-raw material product. Each Kindle novel or work of non-fiction is, at its core, just a series of ones and zeros that is supported by a tiny bit of electricity.

Imagine how expensive it would be to build a list giving away a print version of your book? You have not only the cost of printing it but the shipping, too.

All of this sounds great unless you're just beginning.

Maybe you only have one book and are feeling frustrated that my advice doesn't apply to you. Well, we all had only one book once upon a time.

What I did for my reader magnet for a long time was I wrote a 7,700-word short story that was a standalone thriller. It was different from my mystery book, but it was a bit more of Brian Meeks writing that I thought readers might enjoy. The hope was if they enjoyed *Henry Wood Detective Agency*, they would be interested in the short thriller.

I had it edited and created a cover. I wrote on the cover that it was a 30-minute thriller, so they would know this wasn't a full-blown novel. It's important to set expectations. I didn't want anyone to be upset at the length.

Yes, even something that's free can still piss people off if they're disappointed because it didn't meet expectations.

So, the things you'll need to consider when setting up your reader magnet is the details in making the whole system work.

It starts with a link in the front and back matter of your book telling the reader of the offer. That link needs to go somewhere. I have landing pages for each of my three different lists.

A moment of discussion about the landing pages. It's important that those pages not have any other links or buttons that might distract your potential subscriber. That means there aren't links back to the beginning of your blog. It also means that putting in links to other books you may have written is also a bad idea. If they want more books by you, they've got the links in the book they just read. At this point you want them to subscribe. That's goal number one.

You're giving them two options. Click on the button Join My Reader Group (remember: *never* "subscribe to my Newsletter") or click to close the browser.

Once they click a box comes up that asks for their email address: *Where would you like me to email your copy of (title of the book)?*

It's important to understand that people don't like to give out their email addresses. If you have a box asking for the email address on the first page it will cause some resistance. If the potential subscriber has just taken an action like clicking on the button, they've passed the point of committing. Now, you're just trying to do as they wish, but you still need to know where to send it. At this point, in their mind it is only logical that the email address would be required and their reticence is gone.

What happens next is interesting. The pop up box where they entered the email address is something created by the email service you use. Many people like MailChimp, I use ActiveCampaign (Honorée uses and loves AWeber), which is more expensive but has some nice features.

I began with MailChimp, though, and they have made it easy to setup your mailing list, which also includes the code you'll need to create the little box for gathering the email.

Imagine you've built a nice landing page that had enticing ad copy based upon what you learned from reading Sugarman's *AdWeek* book. You've called the button Join Your Book Title's Reader Group, and the email capture form comes up after that. How does the book get to the reader?

That's the question that stumped me for a while. What I did starting out was to include a link to a Dropbox folder that had the MOBI (Kindle), EPUB (other digital platforms), and PDF versions of the book that readers could then download. That works just fine, but now there's a better way. It's called BookFunnel and Honorée mentioned it earlier. This is a service that delivers your book for you and it's wonderful. I use BookFunnel now.

There is only one more thing about your list. It's crucial that you understand the importance of keeping in touch with your readers. Remember, they like your writing and want to know what's going on. This is an area where I've dropped the ball and I can tell you from experience that some people will forget who you are if you don't remind them from time to time. They may have signed up because of the reader magnet, they may have even enjoyed the free book you sent them, but if it is six months before they hear a peep out of you, they'll have forgotten who you are and won't be as inclined to take an action, such as buy your new book.

It can be hard to get over the feeling you're being annoying, but most people won't be bothered by updates if they're not more than once or twice per month. Doing this will keep your list fresh.

When you're comfortable with all of this list stuff, you can start to consider building an auto-responder campaign that helps during the early stages of having a new subscriber. It's basically a series of evergreen emails that would be of interest to the new subscriber, that keeps you in their mind.

THE LONG GAME

When one is beginning, the focus is on adding readers one at a time. That's normal and there's value in doing that hard work. It's a time where we get over any insecurity we might have about asking someone to try our book. This is when we learn that asking someone if they would like to give our book a read isn't such a big deal.

Back when I had only one book out, I spent a lot of time on Twitter. I wasn't there because I thought it would sell a ton of books, I was there because (in those days) people would just hang out and talk about things. I'd have conversations with my Twitter friend in Malaysia about Liverpool F.C. There would be chats with the guinea pig, BiggusPiggus, about the travel business run by his humans. I follow a lot of guinea pigs! There would be discussions with bloggers about how to build our audience. It wasn't about always selling.

One day a woman that I had barely talked to, tweeted out, "I've just finished a book and need something new to read. Any suggestions?"

> At this point, I was still a little shy about asking, so I eased into it. "What type of genres do you like to read?"

> "I like everything."

"Do you like mysteries?" I asked, hopefully.

"I love mysteries."

"I've written a mystery called the *Henry Wood Detective Agency*. Would you like a link so you could check it out?"

"Yes, please."

I zipped over to Amazon, got the link, and then tweeted it back to her. About five minutes later, I got a tweet back. It read, "I've bought your book and read the first chapter. I love it!"

That's one sale. It's not a big deal, but at the time it was huge. Back then I had many days without sales so each one was treasured. That wasn't the amazing part, though. It was the moment that I realized that we (authors) live in the most incredible time to be publishing our stories.

In a span of less than ten minutes, from my computer in Martelle, Iowa (pop. 252), I made a sales pitch, closed the deal, *and* had the product delivered to the customer—who lived in Antigua. If that same conversation had been between Samuel E. Clemens (Mark Twain) and a woman in Antigua, it would have been by mail. It would have taken months for the back and forth and then still more time to deliver the book.

This realization made me feel unstoppable. Anything was possible. All I needed to do was continue to work and I'd figure out ways to get my books in the hands of readers.

And, all you need to do is continue to work, continue to write, and discover even more ways to get *your* books in the hands of readers!

THE TIME HAS COME

HONORÉE HERE.

The purpose of this book is not just to give you a whole bunch of ideas. The purpose of this book is to give you a whole bunch of ideas that you use, ideas that create a spark and birth other ideas—all of which you deploy with great success. If Brian and I have done our job well, we've inspired you with our ideas and our ideas have done a Vulcan mind-meld with some of your ideas, spawning new and even better ideas. Hopefully, you have been inspired and have already started penciling in some ninja secrets that will cause us to exclaim, *That is genius!*

The best part about ideas is that once they start coming, they come fast and furious. They won't all be gold-star gems of brilliance, and that's okay. Because you've taken the time to add intention and purpose to your direction, you'll most likely be able to sort through our ideas and the ones you have, then you can choose the best ones for you to use right now.

I have shared with you my favorites, and now I'm putting on my coaching hat with the goal of getting you into action. So, before you read any further, grab a pen and some paper, your Bullet Journal, or start a new Evernote document, and together let's craft a finding readers plan for you.

I want you to find and attract new readers as soon as tomorrow, or even today! So let's hurry up and get your plan in place, identify the ninja ideas you think will work best, and get you on the road to finding more readers fast.

When you're ready, turn the page …

Your Action Plan

Honorée here.

Now that you've identified what you want from your writing, you can get down to the business of creating your very own action plan, which you can populate with your numbers and intended action items.

I've used big numbers in this plan on purpose—because I'm a big thinker and I believe in abundance. If at any time the numbers seem too big or overwhelming, *simply change them.* You may not want to do anything more than make enough to be a full-time writer, and that's fantastic. Doing what you love isn't all about the money; it's mostly about being able to make enough money to do what you love. Your first Action Plan could be to make $1,000 a month, instead of $10,000, so you'll just divide all of the numbers by 10. Start where you are, make incremental increases as desired, rinse and repeat. Fair enough? Keep this in mind: in 2008, I made $28.00 on Kindle (thank you, GetBookReport.com!). Everyone starts somewhere, so just begin where you are, and take it from there.

On the flip side, perhaps you are among those who have already made $10,000 a month and are looking to go to your next level. Good for you! This action plan works just as well for scaling up, regardless of the intended size of your business or income.

Your Action Plan

I've provided an example to get you started:

2017 ACTION PLAN EXAMPLE

What I want from my writing: *I am a full-time prosperous author earning in excess of $10,000 per month from my writing.*

Goal #1: $120,000 2016 income = $10,000 per month

Goal #2: 95 total e-books sold per day

Action Items:

1. Do one podcast interview every three days (122 total)

2. Add 5000 people to my author email list (13.69 per day)

3. Update opt-in

4. Revise *Autoresponder Madness* sequence

5. Have twice daily updates in private FB group

6. Post on personal timeline 4x/week

7. One blog post per week

8. Read top 100 other books in my genre, write reviews on Amazon/Goodreads

9. Leave postcards in various locations (elevators, bookstores, etc.)

10. Write 2000 wpd in current WIP to keep with my schedule (730,000 words)

You can download a blank version here: HonoreeCorder.com/FindingReaders.

Go Get 'em, Writer!

Brian and I sincerely hope you take the time to create your Action Plan. Mostly, we want you to execute it! Many an awesome plan has collected dust instead of coming to life, and in your case, that would be tragic! We know that because you not only bought this book, you took the time (your most precious resource) to read it, and probably have started, if not finished, your own Action Plan.

Just as we want you to create and execute your plan, we want your words to find life and the readers who will love them. We encourage you to shed any limiting beliefs that stand in your way, tune into (and turn up!) the inner voice that is cheering you on, and go for it 100%.

Prosperity for Writers, both the book and the course, can help you to eliminate any beliefs you have that aren't serving you (you'll find links in the Resources Section at the back of this book for both, as well as all of our other books).

The only thing standing between you and the readers who will be delighted to find you is, well, not a thing. Rock on, and be sure to write us and let us know how it's going!

Resources

LINKS TO OTHER BOOKS IN THE PROSPEROUS WRITER SERIES:

Prosperity for Writers: A Writer's Guide to Creating Abundance
(The Prosperous Writer Series Book 1)
http://tinyurl.com/ProsperityforWriters

Prosperity for Writers Productivity Journal: A Writer's Workbook for Creating Abundance
http://tinyurl.com/P4WJournal

The Nifty 15: Write Your Book in Just 15 Minutes a Day
(The Prosperous Writer Series Book 2)
http://tinyurl.com/Nifty15

The Prosperous Writer's Guide to Making More Money: Habits, Strategies, and Tactics for Making a Living as a Writer
(The Prosperous Writer Series Book 3)
http://tinyurl.com/AuthorMoney3

LINKS TO OUR READER GROUPS & OTHER AWESOMESAUCENESS:

The Prosperous Writer Mastermind:
HonoreeCorder.com/Writers

***The Prosperous Writer's Guide to Finding Readers* Bonuses:**
HonoreeCorder.com/FindingReaders

BEST BOOK BUSINESS READS:

Sell More Books with Less Social Media: Spend Less Time Marketing and More Time Writing (Chris Syme)
http://tinyurl.com/LessSocialMedia

Text Me! Snap Me! Ask Me Anything!: How Entrepreneurs, Consultants And Artists Can Use The Power of Intimate Attention To Build Their Brand, Grow Their Business And Change The World (Kevin Kruse)
http://tinyurl.com/TextMeSnapMe

The AdWeek Copywriting Handbook: The Ultimate Guide to Writing Powerful Advertising and Marketing Copy from One of America's Top Copywriters (Joseph Sugarman)
http://tinyurl.com/AdWeekCopy

*Reader Magnets: Build Your Author Platform and
Sell more Books on Kindle* (Nick Stephenson)
http://tinyurl.com/ReaderMagnet

On Writing: A Memoir of the Craft (Stephen King)
http://tinyurl.com/SKingOnWriting

*Your First 1000 Copies: The Step-by-Step Guide to
Marketing Your Book* (Tim Grahl)
http://tinyurl.com/First1000Copies

*You Must Write a Book: Boost Your Brand, Get
More Business, and Become the Go-To Expert*
(Honorée Corder)
http://tinyurl.com/YouMustWriteaBook

*The Miracle Morning for Writers: How to Build
a Writing Ritual That Increases Your Impact
and Your Income* (Hal Elrod & Steve Scott, with
Honorée Corder)
http://tinyurl.com/MM4Writers

WRITING AND SELF-PUBLISHING PODCASTS TO LISTEN TO:

*Authors' note: There are so many great podcasts, this is not the full
list, just a few of our favorites to get you started.*

The Author Biz Podcast
TheAuthorBiz.com

The Author Hangout
BookMarketingTools.com/blog

The Self-Publishing Podcast
SterlingandStone.net/podcasts

The Sell More Books Show
SellMoreBooksShow.com

The Smarty Pants Book Marketing Podcast
SmartyPantsBookMarketing.libsyn.com/podcast

The Wordslinger Podcast
KevinTumlinson.com/podcast-rss

The Writer Files Podcast
Rainmaker.fm

QUICK FAVOR

We're wondering, did you enjoy this book?

First of all, thank you for reading our book! May we ask a quick favor?

Will you take a moment to leave an honest review for this book on Amazon? Reviews are the BEST way to help others purchase the book.

You can go to the link below and write your thoughts. We appreciate you!

HonoreeCorder.com/FindingReadersReview

GRATITUDE

GENERAL THANKS

To my husband, partner, and best friend, Byron.

To my daughter and inspiration, Lexi, I'm so grateful to be your mom.

To my mastermind peeps, Rich, Andrea, and Brian ~ I'm so grateful for your support, ideas, and our synergy.

WHO IS HONORÉE

Honorée Corder is the author of dozens of books, including *You Must Write a Book, Prosperity for Writers* and *The Prosperous Writer* book series, *Vision to Reality, Business Dating, The Successful Single Mom* book series, *If Divorce is a Game, These are the Rules,* and *The Divorced Phoenix.* She is also Hal Elrod's business partner in *The Miracle Morning* book series. Honorée coaches business professionals, writers, and aspiring non-fiction authors who want to publish their books to bestseller status, create a platform, and develop multiple streams of income. She also does all sorts of other magical things, and her badassery is legendary. You can find out more at HonoreeCorder.com.

Honorée Enterprises, Inc.
Honoree@HonoreeCorder.com
http://www.HonoreeCorder.com
Twitter: @Honoree
& @Singlemombooks
Facebook: http://www.facebook.com/Honoree

WHO IS BRIAN

Brian D. Meeks (sometimes Arthur Byrne) is a full-time author who writes fiction under his name and the name of his protagonist from *Underwood, Scotch, and Wry*, Arthur Byrne. He has released 12 novels, with the 13th on the way. In addition to mysteries, thrillers, YA, science fiction, and satire, he writes non-fiction with his co-author Honorée Corder about the business of writing and publishing. He lives in Iowa, travels whenever he can, and follows lots of guinea pigs on Facebook because they are freaking adorable.

EcocandleRiel@gmail.com

THE PROSPEROUS WRITER
BOOK SERIES

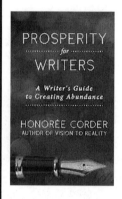

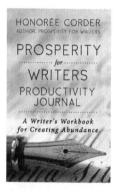

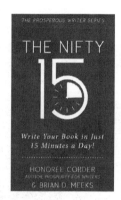

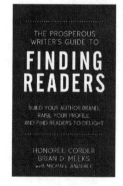

COMING SOON ...

The Prosperous Writer Mindset

Made in the USA
Lexington, KY
13 June 2017